T0362916

PUBLISHED BY BOOM BOOKS

www.boombooks.biz

ABOUT THIS SERIES

.... But after that, I realised that I knew very little about these parents of mine. They had been born about the start of the Twentieth Century, and they died in 1970 and 1980. For their last 20 years, I was old enough to speak with a bit of sense.

I could have talked to them a lot about their lives. I could have found out about the times they lived in. But I did not. I know almost nothing about them really. Their courtship? Working in the pits? The Lock-out in the Depression? Losing their second child? Being dusted as a miner? The shootings at Rothbury? My uncles killed in the War? Love on the dole? There were hundreds, thousands of questions that I would now like to ask them. But, alas, I can't. It's too late.

Thus, prompted by my guilt, I resolved to write these books. They describe happenings that affected people, real people. The whole series is, to coin a modern phrase, designed to push your buttons, to make you remember and wonder at things forgotten. The books might just let nostalgia see the light of day, so that oldies and youngies will talk about the past and re-discover a heritage otherwise forgotten. Hopefully, they will spark discussions between generations, and foster the asking and answering of questions that should not remain unanswered.

BORN IN 1959?
WHAT ELSE HAPPENED?

RON WILLIAMS

AUSTRALIAN SOCIAL HISTORY

BOOK 21 IN A SERIES OF 35
FROM 1939 to 1973

War Babies Years (1939 to 1945):   7 Titles
Baby Boom Years (1946 to 1960):   15 Titles
Post Boom Years (1961 to 1972):   13 Titles

BOOM, BOOM BABY, BOOM

PUBLISHED BY BOOM BOOKS
Wickham, NSW, Australia

Web: www.boombooks.biz
Email: jen@boombooks.biz

© Ron Williams 2012   This printing 2023

Creator: Williams, Ron, 1934- author
ISBN:9780994601599 (paperback)
Series: Born in series, book 21.
Almanacs, Australian.
Australia--History--Miscellanea--20th century.
Dewey Number: 994.04

Cover images: National Archives of Australia.
A1200, L16165, William Dobell;
A1200, L29817, rabbiting;
A1200, L33480, family watching TV;
A12111, 1/1959/4/13 fish markets.

CONTENTS

IMPORTANT PEOPLE AND EVENTS

Queen of England	Elizabeth II
Prime Minister of Australia	Bob Menzies
Leader of Opposition	Doc Evatt
Governor General	William McKell
Pope	John XXIII
US President	Dwight Eisenhower
PM of Britain	Harold Macmillan

WINNER OF THE ASHES

1956	England 2 - 1
1958-59	Australia 4 - 0
1961	Australia 2 - 1

MELBOURNE CUP WINNERS

1958	Baystone
1959	Macdougal
1960	Hi Jinx

ACADEMY AWARDS 1959

Best Actor	Charlton Heston
Best Actress	Simone Signoret
Best Movie	Ben Hur

PREFACE TO THIS SERIES: 1939 TO 1972

This book is the 21st in a series of books that I have researched and written. It tells a story about a number of important or newsworthy Australia-centric events that happened in 1959. The series covers each of the years from 1939 to 1973, for a total of thirty-five books.

I developed my interest in writing these books a few years ago at a time when my children entered their teens. My own teens started in 1947, and I started trying to remember what had happened to me then. I thought of the big events first, like Saturday afternoon at the pictures, and cricket in the back yard, and the wonderful fun of going to Maitland on the train for school each day. Then I recalled some of the not-so-good things. I was an altar boy, and that meant three or four Masses a week. I might have thought I loved God at that stage, but I really hated his Masses. And the schoolboy bullies, like Greg Farrell, and the hapless Freddie Evans. Yet, to compensate for these, there was always the beautiful, black headed, blue-sailor-suited June Brown, who I was allowed to worship from a distance.

I also thought about my parents. Most of the major events that I lived through came to mind readily. But after that, I realised that I really knew very little about these parents of mine. They had been born about the start of the Twentieth Century, and they died in 1970 and 1980. For their last 20 years, I was old enough to speak with a bit of sense. I could have talked to them a lot about their lives. I could have found out about the times they lived in. But I did not. I know almost nothing about them really. Their courtship? Working in the pits? The Lock-out in the Depression?

Losing their second child? Being dusted as a miner? The shootings at Rothbury? My uncles killed in the War? There were hundreds, thousands of questions that I would now like to ask them. But, alas, I can't. It's too late.

Thus, prompted by my guilt, I resolved to write these books. They describe happenings that affected people, real people. In **1959,** there is some coverage of international affairs, but a lot more on the Billy Grahame crusade. There's nothing on Billy Hughes's populist posturing, but plenty on the Kingsgrove Slasher. The whole series is, to coin a modern phrase, designed to push the reader's buttons, to make you remember and wonder at things forgotten. The books might just let nostalgia see the light of day, so that oldies and youngies will talk about the past and re-discover a heritage otherwise forgotten. Hopefully, they will spark discussions between generations, and foster the asking and the answering of questions that should not remain unanswered.

The sources of my material. I was born in 1934, so that I can remember well a great deal of what went on around me from 1946 onwards. But of course, the bulk of this book's material came from research. That meant that I spent many hours at various public libraries reading microfilms of newspapers, magazines, periodicals and so on. My task here was to sift out day-by-day those stories and events that would be of interest to the most readers. Then I supplemented these with materials from books, broadcasts, memoirs, biographies, government reports and statistics, Ministers' statements, and the like. And I talked to old-timers, one-on-one, and in organized groups, and to Baby Boomers about their recollections. People with stories to tell come out of the woodwork, and talk no end about the tragic and funny and commonplace events that have shaped their lives.

The presentation of each book. For each year covered, the end result is a collection of short Chapters on many of the topics that concerned ordinary people in that year. I think I have covered most of the major issues that people then were interested in. On the other hand, in some cases I have dwelt a little on minor frivolous matters, perhaps to the detriment of more sober considerations. Still, in the long run, this makes the book more readable, and hopefully it will convey adequately the spirit of the times.

Each of the books is mainly Sydney based, but I have been deliberately national in outlook, so that readers elsewhere will feel comfortable that I am talking about matters that affected them personally. After all, housing shortages and strikes and a tuberculosis epidemic involved all Australians, and other issues, such as problems overseas, had no State component in them. Overall, I expect I can make you wonder, remember, rage and giggle equally, no matter where you hail from.

HAPPY LEADERS IN EARLY 1959

The year 1959 got off to a remarkable start. For a decade, at the beginning of each New Year, world leaders had bombarded us with messages of good cheer and hope for the future. But there were also dire warnings that we faced a number of crises that would gut us, and with the added implied message that we would survive only if we were smart enough to do everything that they told us to do. For example, since Prime Minister Bob Menzies came to power in 1950, he had told us time and again that we faced dreadful consequences if the forces of international Communism were not destroyed, and that if we wanted to avoid this disaster, we would have to rout the few but powerful Communists on the local scene.

This year it was very different. The bon homme and hope were there as usual. But **the Bob Menzies Doomsday messages were nowhere to be seen**.

I remain convinced of two things. One is that the Communist Powers, though still ruthless and predatory, have growing internal reasons for not deliberately provoking a world war.

The second is that the American recession seems to be lifting rapidly, while the growing strength of Britain's currency, Stirling, will provide further stimulus to world trade. These latter circumstances should before long bring benefits to our own country. 1959 is to be entered with optimistic determination and true Australian confidence.

Dr Evatt, the Leader of the Federal Opposition, talked like a new man. He extolled the virtues of conciliation and arbitration in local disputes, and went on to recommend them for international arguments.

The United Nations and its Charter are the instruments chosen by the nations of the world to indicate and regulate the procedures of settlement. Setbacks occur in this field, but I know there is a far stronger tendency today **to resort to conciliation than has ever occurred before**. Some very important steps have been made by agreement between the East and West during the year. If this continues, the great objectives of peace on earth and goodwill to all men may gradually be attained.

What was going on here? Menzies without his threats of war? Evatt without his long list of Government's faults? It's hard to credit. I know it is the New Year, and everyone puts on a nice face. But can leopards really change their spots? They haven't in the past. Well, let's try Joe Cahill, the Premier of NSW. Surely, he will come up with a litany of complaints about how the Commonwealth is swindling the States out of their fair share of revenue.

Nature has been kind to us. We garnered a bountiful wheat harvest and the wool clip is expected to be a near record. Production in secondary industry is also expected to be at record levels, and many new industries, backed by overseas capital, are making a worthy contribution.

We have every reason to look to the future with the fullest degree of confidence. The economy of NSW was never more sound, and there are no serious problems looming that will put a brake on our prosperity.

I am sure that we will begin the New Year in a spirit of **gratitude** and with complete confidence in the future.

Gratitude? Coming from Joe Cahill? Wonders will never cease. Perhaps if we look overseas we can find some evidence of dissonance. No good looking to Queen Elizabeth, because her Message is always full of wholesome optimism, with no political or critical elements at all. What about America? After the fiascos of the war with the Reds in Korea in the early fifties, and the Suez Crisis in 1956, and the Red invasion of Hungary in the same year, surely some good old-fashioned animosity will be semaphored.

But, what a disappointment. In the US, all things were light and beautiful with the Russians. At that very moment, the Soviet Deputy Prime Minister, Menshikov, was making a visit, and was being feted by the President, General Eisenhower, and the Congress. And behind him, in Russia, the Soviet Premier, Mr Nikita Khrushchev, was broadcasting that "the solution to the world's problems depends on the people of the world, and no nation desires peace more than Russia. From the bottom of our hearts, we the Soviet people wish the American people well-being, happiness, and a life of peace and tranquility for 1959."

Now, of course, I give up. Obviously there is no chance of finding anyone who has not been affected by the excess of goodwill that 1959 began with. Surely there was some pragmatic official somewhere who would say "Cut it out, mate. You will all be back bickering and posturing in a month's time." But, no there was not.

Then again, perhaps it is me that is wrong. Perhaps, the world **is** suddenly a better place, and all the problems of the world will soon be ironed out, and 1959 will go down in History as the year when it all started. What a lovely idea.

Somehow, I would bet against it. Probably 1959 will bring its share of ineptitude and strife, and personal worries, just like other years previously. Still, there is no point in guessing, so it's better to get on with this book.

Let me just add that I hope that the year **does** turn out to be special for all the 59-ers, and that each of you readers finds it a most happy and prosperous year indeed.

BACKGROUND PROBLEMS FROM 1958

The first of these was the never-ending range of strikes that was offered to the public. Almost every day, some trade unionists would call on a strike, and deny to householders the electricity or gas or trains or ice or meat or what-have-you that they needed. The strikers wanted better or safer conditions, or more pay, or a day off at the races. The strikes might last for the day, or a week or rarely for a few months. In any case, they were a real pain in the neck to the ordinary citizens and as constant as the northern star.

The second problem was the Cold War. The United States and Russia were quite happily furthering their own political purposes by fostering hatred of each other. So they were posturing and threatening each other in dozens of nations round the world, and swamping the locals with endless streams of propaganda. At the moment, major conflicts were not on the agenda, but the animosity was still a big factor and an ever-present factor in international relations.

A third problem was that the Brits were talking more and more about joining into a common market with Europe. If they did ever that, it would jolt Australia out of our comfortable trade relationships with Britain, and force us to seek markets elsewhere. This could have serious consequences for our wool, wheat, and other agricultural products. At the moment, it was getting harder for us to turn a blind eye, and how it might end was uncertain and worrying to some. Though it must be said that most of our folk remained not very interested in overseas matters, and a good percentage lost no sleep at all over our coming trade prospects.

BLESSINGS FROM 1958

Australia had many blessings at the start of 1959, and I want to point to **just one**. I will illustrate this by reference to the rest of the world.

Many, many other nations were wracked with revolutions against former imperial white powers, or against new local black tyrants, or towards the creation of the new ideological regimes backed by the USA or Communism. Many of them had racial riots, extremes of poverty, poor education and health, and were suffering from active class systems. **Australia missed out on all these torments.**

You can add that we were well educated, had a health system that was as good as any, had an adequate security blanket for unfortunates, had high employment, could all afford a good house eventually, had cosmetics at the counter and beer in the fridge, and there will be another barbi next Sunday.

SOME EVENTS FROM 1958

The biggest news story of 1958 concerned a father and son surnamed Hursey. They were wharfies who refused to pay a levy to the Wharf Workers Federation Union to support Labour candidates at coming Federal elections. They were harassed and bullied for months, and so too were their families. They won a Court case in the Tasmanian Supreme Court that said the levy was illegal and the Federation was fined a few thousand Pounds.

Despite this, they were still physically pushed around, and the other wharfies refused to work with them. They gave up when the violence towards their families got too great.

The other conspicuous series of events involved the churches. They got involved in all sorts of disputes, and in all of them ended up with vicious public in-fighting among themselves. They did no credit to themselves.

One episode stemmed from the Christian Brothers, an Order of the Catholic Church. This group decided to buy a historic and popular pub in Sydney's Manly. This did not sit well with the Protestant codes. Then they decided to raffle it, to the general public. The sins of gambling and drinking were too much for the opposition clergy, and the Letters pages of the newspapers erupted.

But the Churches became involved over other matters such as birth control, accusations that Sunday Schools were scaring hell out of children, and their opposition to Sunday sports and paid entertainment on Sundays. In all of these, they ended at odds with the general population.

WE ARE ALMOST READY FOR 1959

I can tell you in advance that there is nothing much to worry about. Nothing really terrible happened. Economic conditions were pretty good, people had their brand new TV's, and everyone felt prosperous enough to get themselves deeply into debt, Unions were always striking, public transport and roads were all terrible, and rabbits were a menace. In short, for most people, for most of the time, things were normal. Still, Baby Boomers were producing their offspring, advances in technology were changing old patterns of behaviour, and people were becoming more confident and adventurous. So, this 1959 year ahead might turn out to be one of stability, but also one of excitement and involvement. **I hope you enjoy living it**.

But just before we go, I will list my rules in writing these books. This might help you as you go along.

MY RULES IN WRITING THESE BOOKS

NOTE. Throughout this book, I rely a lot on re-producing **Letters from the newspapers.** Whenever I do this, I put the text in a different font, and indent it a little, and make the font somewhat smaller. **I do not edit the text at all**. That is, I do not correct spelling or grammar. **If the text gets at all garbled, I do not correct it.** It's just as it was seen in the daily Papers and other publications .

SECOND NOTE. The material for this book, when it comes from newspapers, is reported as it was seen at the time. **If** the benefit of hindsight over the years changes things, then I **might** record that in my **Comments**. The info reported thus reflects matters **as they were seen by readers in 1959.**

THIRD NOTE. Let me also apologise in advance to anyone I might offend. In a work such as this, it is certain some people will think I got some things wrong. I am sure that I did, but please remember, all of this is **only my opinion**. And really, **my opinion does not matter one little bit in the scheme of things. I hope you will say "silly old bugger", and shrug your shoulders, and read on till the end.**

So, now we really are ready. Here we go.

JANUARY: MARRIAGE TO ASIANS

Ten years ago, any mention of any sort of co-operation or fraternisation with Asians was repugnant to vast numbers of Australians. While hatred of the Japanese as a race was paramount as a consequence of the War, it was the unhappy lot of **all** Asians to be treated as pariahs on Australian soil.

What a remarkable difference ten years makes. When you look at January's news stories, you notice that Jack McEwan, the Minister for Trade, was hosting a Japanese Trade Fair at the Sydney Trocadero. There, he praised the trade agreement we made with Japan two years earlier, and pointed to the large amount of goods that were now flowing between the two countries. At another level, Japanese models were visiting Sydney, and parading the wares of their nation. Such goings-on a decade earlier would have offended most of the population.

Sir Macfarlane Burnett was thus on fairly safe ground when he advocated marriages between Australians and non-Europeans. Burnett was a respected Professor from the Australian National University in Canberra, in medical science, and he often commented on public affairs. In this case, he was recommending that such marriages should be encouraged because he thought that they would improve **this nation's gene pool**. He conceded that this might gradually means that Australians would develop a different skin tone and body shape, and could see no objection to this. But, as he pointed out, no nation could hope to survive if it tried to maintain itself as some sort of "pure" citadel, having no interaction with outsiders.

His views came at a time of changing attitudes towards Asians. The White Australia policy was being quietly dismantled. **The "dictation test" had been abolished in 1958**, and over the following two years, regulations were progressively changed to remove some restraints on Asians entering the country. By now, the population accepted that Asians were not in fact inferior to us, as had been often claimed a decade earlier, and could well come to this nation without seriously undermining our values. The same population, however, was not quite ready to advocate mixed-marriages en masse. Thus Burnett's letter, which would have driven many people into a frenzy ten years earlier, passed without response in the Herald, except for two rather matter-of-fact Letters that confined themselves to immersion in the gene pool.

Letters, Ailsa Davies. With reference to Macfarlane Burnett's paper suggesting marriage with non-Europeans: As a kindergarten director for some years I had a good deal of experience with children of Australian-Asian descent. While these children were intelligent and of fairly average physical build, they were consistently marked by a lack of emotional stability.

This seems to indicate that a combination of the temperaments of East and West does not produce a balanced personality.

Letters, Griffith Taylor. It is 40 years since I published my first memoir on race in the "Geographical Review" (New York, 1919). There I showed that each continent contained representatives of the four original major races. In Europe, for instance, racial mixing between distinct races has been in evidence throughout history, without notable racial or cultural disadvantages. My

1919 classification of races is now discussed at length in various anthropological manuals, such as those by Cole and Count in the United States.

In 1919, I concluded that the Alpine race, occupying Eastern Europe and most of Asia, was the latest major race to evolve. I cannot see how any biological harm can result from inter-marriage between Australians and Asian, such as Chinese, Japanese, or many Indian and Indonesian nationals. Social troubles due to differences in culture will naturally occur; but racial prejudice will vanish as scientific knowledge replaces current ethnological ignorance.

I rejoice to find Australian scientists (such as Sir Macfarlane Burnet and Dr Ian Hogbin), for almost the first time, supporting what I have taught for the last 40 years.

CUBA IN TURMOIL

One person who would not agree that peace and harmony were in the offing was Fidel Castro, who on New Year's Day made his long-expected move to take over government in Cuba.

News item, Havana, January 2ⁿᵈ. President Batista left Cuba tonight, en route to the Dominican Republic. His wife and children and his Cabinet also left, with the US as their destination. A three-man junta, under the command of General Cantilo, took over the government.

The move by Batista was made because he expects that **rebel leader Fidel Castro** will invade the capital, and attempt to set up a new rule. It is expected Castro will be supported by a general strike, which is expected to start in a few hours. Police in Havana have begun to set up barriers to intercept Castro's forces, which are believed to number 4000 well-trained and well-armed soldiers.

The rebels profess to want solely to oust Batista. The US, on the other hand, suspect that they are supported and financed by Russia and China, and want to establish a Soviet-style republic on the very door-step of the US. Castro and his rebels have been waging a guerrilla-style warfare against Batista's army for two years, and it is thought that they now have the might to topple Batista.

News item, Havana, January 4th. Dr Manual Urritia last night took the oath of office as Cuba's provisional President. The moves to oust Batista had proceeded almost without bloodshed, and the new Government was named and sworn in as a result.

Fidel Castro, and his army, are on the way to Havana, but are being delayed by tumultuous welcomes as they pass through the countryside. It was announced that Castro's position would be "Delegate of the President for the Armed Forces", which means he will be the Chief of the Armed Forces. Some sources expect that he might not be happy with that role.

A few weeks later, President Urritia resigned, and Castro was then left in sole control, and **assumed the role of Prime Minister**. He quickly set about **appropriating American sugar plantations**, without consultation with the US, and without adequate compensation. At this stage, he was not inclined to Communism. Rather, he appeared to crave the limelight of the capitalist world, and within a month was strutting the stage in Washington. But in the meantime, his flamboyant new regime was raising eyebrows over his activities at home.

News item, Havana, January 23rd. Army colonel Jesus Blanco was brought to trial yesterday in Havana's

Sports Palace Stadium as an alleged war criminal. The atmosphere was reminiscent of the Roman Colosseum in that the Stadium was packed tight with spectators who jeered and whistled and hooted throughout the trial. The event was shown on TV, and broadcast over the radio. The trial lasted four hours, after which he was found guilty. He was executed a few days later. Blanco was on trial for having tortured and murdered 108 Castro followers. Over the course of January, an estimated 500 former Batista supporters were tried and executed.

Comment. After this first extravaganza, similar trials were conducted in proper courts, with somewhat more conservative proceedings. Castro was at this stage disliked by the US, but not yet a sworn enemy. It took him **a couple of years to reach that exalted status**.

We will hear more about Fidel in later months.

IS MECKIFF A CHUCKER?

The Test Cricket Series was well under way, with Australia, as usual, giving the Poms a good licking. By the middle of January, we were on the point of winning the third match in the Series, and thereby regaining the Ashes, which England had won from us on our last Tour there by various dubious and nefarious means, including fielding a better team.

At this stage, a number of English cricket writers claimed that our very good fast bowler, Ian Meckiff, **was throwing, and not bowling, the ball**. Let me say, as a small aside, that the rivalry between the cricket sides of the two countries was very intense, and sometimes bitter. But it was nothing compared to the rivalry between the opposing sets of sports writers, who would do anything to get a headline that at the same time defames the other team. This, of course, is part of the grand game of cricket, and adds considerably to the finest traditions of sportsmanship with which the game is synonymous.

In any case, this vile accusation was stoutly denied by the Australian Press, which pointed out that the complaint came only from the English **Press**, and not from their team. It is a matter that I hardly think bears further discussion, other than to say I have examined Meckiff's bowling action and that shows beyond that the man's arm is as straight as can be. After all, the man **is** Australian.

AUSTRALIA - USSR RELATIONS

As I mentioned earlier, the Soviet Deputy Prime Minister, Menshevik, had succeeded in his good-will tour of America. But it turned a little sour just as he was due to leave. On the eve of his departure, he had a bust-up with an Undersecretary for Trade, in official talks on liberalising trade between the two countries. During the discussions he told the Americans that all they were interested in doing was placing spies into Russia, and that the US was not interested in joining in trade. The American, Douglas Dillon, in reply, said that Menshevik was fatuous, and showed a lack of respect for the people who had received him with open arms.

Comment. Maybe, the spirit of the New Year would **not** last. In any case, it was evident a new diplomatic move was under way. In 1956, in the Petrov crisis, Australia and USSR had played tit-for-tat by breaking off diplomatic relations with each other. Now, there were signs aplenty that we two nations would soon re-establish those relations.

I do not recall sleeping any better when I heard this, but it does seem better for nations to talk rather than sulk.

TV NEWS

Channel Seven last night made television history when the cities of Sydney and Melbourne were connected directly to the simultaneous viewing of the one programme. Viewers in both cities were able to watch Johnny Parkinson sing a trial song at the same time. This demonstration was a test for the direct telecast of the cricket tomorrow, and it was hailed as a success.

The three Sydney channels will receive the telecast from Melbourne, and will show it for two hours each day. If the operation is a success, and receives viewer support, it is expected that the hours of broadcast will be increased.

NEWS AND VIEWS

On the Beach. The film, "On the Beach", based on the novel by Nevil Shute, was to be made in Melbourne soon. It told the story of an Atom Bomb attack on the world, and there were only a very few survivors. Two of these lucky people were Fred Astaire and Ava Gardner. They arrived a few days apart, and were welcomed at Sydney airport by adoring fans. Gregory Peck, another survivor, had his own fan club greet him a week later.

News item, Rome. Pope John XXIII announced today that he would **summon an Ecumenical Council of all Catholic Bishops** to consider matters pertaining to the governance of the Church. He advised that he would be inviting members of other Christian faiths, as well as non-Christian churches.

Comment. This quiet announcement heralded **years of turmoil for the Catholic Church**. The Council suggested many reforms and over a period of thirty years, some of them were adopted while others were stymied. As a result, the Church is now split between a conservative element, that loosely approximates the pre-Council, while the Liberals are closer to post-Council in their thinking. But in any case, the homogeneity that marked the pre-Council days has given way to an uncomfortable truce.

News item. Workmen today started **taking up the tram tracks** along George Street in Sydney. They will work each day, Monday to Friday, from 7.30 to 4.15. When the tracks are removed, concrete will be poured into the hole left behind, and the road will be resurfaced. Traffic authorities expect there will be some disruption in Sydney's busiest street.

News Item, Sydney. For the first time in 45 years, NSW had **no deaths from poliomyelitis last year**. In 1913, there were 25 cases reported, but these were found to be other diseases. This current situation shows a huge change from 10 years ago, when polio had reached very severe levels. The change has been brought about by a programme of vaccination for children and others on a large scale. The reduction in the incidence of the disease was a huge weight off the minds of parents, who lived in silent dread of the disease striking their children.

News item, Melbourne. The national chaplain of the Catholic Youth Movements tonight spoke out about **the dangers of rock 'n roll**. "Many youths, boys and girls, claim the very rhythm has for them a sensual effect and, therefore, it is more difficult to maintain one's poise and respect. Indeed, instances of where boys lose their respect for girls are legion. With the loss of this respect, we find that girls lose their own self respect, so essential to preserve the morals of our youth. Worst of all is the freedom of movement of both parties. Youth should seek healthy entertainments where dignified restraint is the accepted form."

News item, Washington. The US Senate Racket Committee is currently sitting to investigate the claims that Mafia and others racketeers are moving in on establishments that are selling music through **juke boxes**. These boxes have become very popular, and are providing music to huge numbers of customers. The racketeers allegedly are coercing store-owners to buy records from them, and to play them to the exclusion of all other music. Several store-owners claim to have been bashed and had their stores smashed as they refused to participate in the racket

News item, Sydney. The State Government of NSW is drafting legislation **to test the blood alcohol level of drivers** as a means of determining their innocence or guilt in Court on drink-driving charges. Motorists will not be compelled to take the tests, and they will be purely voluntary. Thus they are expected to be used mainly to establish innocence of the crime.

News item, Eden NSW. Fishermen, on the South Coast bordering Victoria, claim that crayfish fishermen are slaughtering fairy penguins to use them as bait. They say the little birds do not run away from you and the boats just come in and knock them over with sticks. The penguins are then cut down the middle and run through stakes and placed in lobster pots. More than 200 birds were recently killed in the one morning. They make the choicest lobster bait that you can get.

Letters, E Whitely. May I mention my pleasure in reading about the proposed **aerial campaign against flies in Bathurst?** For the first 30 years of my life I rather assumed that flies could not be dealt with effectively and became as complacent as the average Australian. In Central Burma, in 1944-5, the RAF medical authorities showed me what could be done to reduce flies in a matter of weeks by a combination of ground spraying and other measures. I recall that in Malaya and Singapore more was done by communities smaller and otherwise more backward than Sydney.

Whether the overseas methods as they stand would be effective in Australia or not, I cannot say. But I suspect very strongly that we suffer here needlessly.

FEBRUARY: A CALL TO GOD

Dr. Billy Graham. On February 12th, Billy Graham arrived in Sydney, en route to Melbourne. This Doctor of Letters, and of Theology, was a minister of the Baptist Church, and had been an evangelist for the last ten years. That means that the content of his sermons was focused on love of God, and on God's love for humans, so that forgiveness of sins was simply a matter of confession accompanied by a desire to do better in the future. He steered clear of weighty matters, such as the Three Persons One God, and Transubstantiation, and dwelt on man's personal relationship with God.

His style of preaching was foreign to Australia. He was mobile, always moving about, flourishing his arms, and quite ready to raise his voice. He was backed by choirs with jazzy music, and by singers that looked as good as they sang. His **first aim**, in presenting to a big audience, was to whip that willing group into a state of great excitement, and hopefully drive some of them to the point where they would come forward towards the stage, and proclaim publicly that they were repentant sinners determined henceforth to get on the right side of God.

His **second aim** was to have a more lasting effect by convincing the larger audience that they were close to God if they would only reach out, and that they should incorporate God into their everyday world. He called his visit to Australia **a Crusade**, and he intended to leave behind tens of thousands of people proclaiming their active friendship with God.

Graham arrives in Australia. At the airport, he was very discreet. He refused to comment on drinking and gambling in Australia, and said simply "I have just now arrived." He went on to say:

I have come to remind you of old truths, and to learn something about you. I have not come to point a self-righteous finger at the sins of Australia, because we in America have our own sins, and plenty of them. A solution to the great social and political problems of the world is a return to God. If the western world is to survive the challenge of Communism, it must have a spiritual revival.

This was about as bland as you can get, and some of the hundreds of supporters who met him at the airport might have gone home thinking that he was a bit of a fizzer.

There were others who were dubious about the methods used by Graham. He might be just a bit too radical. These views were expressed **before** Graham's tour got under way.

Letters, Frederick Aarons. The participation of the Church of England in the forthcoming high-pressure mission of Dr Graham came as a surprise to a number of professing Anglicans, including this writer. This surprise, coupled with a measure of scepticism, arose partly from the departure from the Church's conservatism; but perhaps more from the nature of a mission of this kind, which seems to rely for success upon the personality of the preacher and his entourage, rather than the intrinsic worth of the subject of discourse.

Surely experience shows that the appeals to "pathos" rather than to "ethos", **to emotions rather than to reason**, must be ephemeral in their reactions, resulting in a fall from elation down to a level of spiritual feeling lower than before. The ideals and doctrines of Christianity are clear and simple, and the province of the Church is to present these in clear and simple terms as far as possible to individuals. One might be excused for asking if the Church feels itself incapable of performing these functions. **It has deserted**, at least temporarily, **the cool shade of reflective reason for the blazing heat of emotionalism.**

Letters, Kathleen Donovan. Frederick Aarons expresses the opinion of many evidently sincere people concerning the Graham mission. They are of this opinion, I believe, because they ask themselves the wrong question, namely, "Do the methods used appeal to me?" The right question, and indeed the question which every Christian must sincerely and prayerfully seek to answer, is this: "Is Billy Graham a chosen vessel of the Lord?"

If he is, then no Christian need be afraid of giving whole-hearted support to the mission. Rather should the Christian fear to withhold such support. My own belief, and that of thousands representing many denominations, is that **the Lord has indeed raised up Billy Graham and is doing a mighty work through him.**

It is not a matter, as Mr Aarons suggests, of the Church feeling incapable of performing its function. It is a matter of the Lord using whom He will. It is true that no man can hinder the work of the Lord, but it is a sad thing that many Christians are missing a great privilege and blessing by dissociating themselves from the Crusade.

Letters, Grahame Hall. It is obvious that the merits of Billy Graham's Crusade cannot be assessed until some three of four months after its completion and, in the light of previous campaigns in Scotland, England and the United States, the results cannot be expected to be of much significance, if any, in regard to increased congregations.

It is assumed that the authorities responsible for the invitation to Dr Graham consulted organisers of previous crusades overseas and weighed up the value of such a campaign in respect to resultant effect upon church attendances. Surely the facts and statistics compiled since these crusades would have given little encouragement to the cause for such activity here.

Graham in Melbourne. Graham's first meeting was marred a little by heavy rain at the Melbourne Stadium. He attracted 35,000 people and **622 persons came forward and made "Decisions" after he spoke**.

The second meeting was more typical, even though it was conducted at the small West Melbourne Stadium. People began queuing four hours before the meeting was due to start. An hour later, with the numbers now around 1,000, the crowd started to sing hymns. By the time he started, the ground was filled to its capacity of 7,500 with another 2,000 people outside watching proceedings on closed circuit television.

He told the audience that the followers of Christ had let the barrier down on Sunday. After all, it was the Lord's Day, but the forces of commercialism and blatant pleasure were taking it over. He stressed that we were living in an era where there was a tremendous emphasis on sex, and that we were tempted at every corner. He went on to beseech young people to honour their elders and their parents. "We are living in a day when the young become lawless and disobedient to their parents."

The musical part of the evening was recorded for a broadcast that would be heard over 1,000 radio stations throughout the world. Part of that recording included a mass choir of 500 volunteers singing *O Lamb of God* quietly in the background as people came forward to "Decide" for Christ. As these people moved forward, Dr Graham intoned that "This is God, not Billy Graham, calling you. It is God the Holy Spirit."

Some of the crowd were surprised at the volume of Graham's voice when he walked away from the microphones. The secret was a new technology involving a tiny microphone clipped to his tie. The wire ran underneath his arm, and out the back of his coat.

His Crusade in Melbourne went on for a month. Despite atrocious weather, that covered the range from heat waves to floods to biting southerlies, he attracted a total audience of over 600,000 people, and that included about 20,000 deciders. Then he moved to Sydney, where we will catch him later.

INDONESIA? WHERE'S THAT

Prior to the end of World War II, Indonesia had been a collection of hundreds of scattered islands, under the control of the Dutch. After the War, **forces for independence from foreign rule had grown rapidly**, until by 1959 most of Indonesia was autonomous, and also most of it had been welded into one single autonomous state. West New Guinea, though, was still under Dutch rule. Now, in 1959, decisions had to be made about the future of this large half-island.

There were three interested parties. **Firstly**, the Dutch. They had withdrawn most of their military and other instruments of the colonial days from Indonesia proper, and were happy enough to hand over West New Guinea.

Second, the Indonesians. They were pleased to accept the new territory, and in fact thought that it should become part of Indonesia, basically because that was how it had been for a very long time. These two nations had been talking together for a couple of years about the situation and had worked out what compensation would be paid, and what to do about maintaining public servants and infrastructure, and the like. This was a virtually settled deal.

Australia was the **third interested party**. There were many different groups who believed that we had a vital interest in this matter. Some, like the Leader of the Labor Party, Dr Evatt, and the RSL, thought that the whole of New Guinea should be put under United Nations mandate, and be administered by Australia. Others were concerned that if Indonesia were to get control of the Western end of the island, we would be cheek to jowl with an Asian neighbour of uncertain performance, and that border troubles would be continuous. Another group worried about the defence aspect, saying that we would be more vulnerable than if the Dutch stayed there. Still another group wanted the natives to be given a vote, to determine for themselves who they wanted as over-lords. There were all sorts of worries and solutions, many of them close to ratbaggery.

In retrospect, all these divergent views had one thing in common. That was that a new nation had suddenly come into being, right on Australia's front doorstep. And, with a touch of paranoia, this was made more salient by the fact that it was an Asian nation. White Australia was not yet dead. And the US was flooding Indonesia with its munitions and weapons left over from the War. So it was easy to raise concerns about a giant and supposedly hostile new nation, only a few hundred miles away, with an unstable government that might any moment turn to Communism, and become belligerent. Nowadays, the frightening picture would have been embellished with many a reference to the fact that the Indonesians were mainly Muslim. But, fortunately, Islam at that time did not present much cause for paranoia.

In the long run, cool heads prevailed. There was clearly no case for Australia to intervene in any way. This was a matter for the Dutch and Indonesian powers, and both of these were very deliberate in extending to Australia the courtesy of asking us for advice. Dr Subandrio, the Indonesian Foreign Affairs Minister, came to Australia to discuss what could be done to protect any interests we had in the Territory. The Dutch were doing the same. Through all the turmoil of ideas, Menzies and External Affairs Minister, Casey, maintained that it was a matter for the other two interested parties to decide. They held that line, in the face of severe criticism from many quarters, including loads of newspapers, until the matter was decided along the lines of non-intervention.

Correspondence was very vocal. A sample is included below

Letters, Frank Glancer. Mr Casey's recent agreement with Mr Subandrio can only be classified as a cynical betrayal of the men whose defence of the Kokoda Trail thrilled us all. These men, the ones still living, risked their lives to be free from overseas tyranny, and now see that tyranny looming again in the shape of Indonesian domination. They did not fight to see the Indonesians replace the Japanese. They fought to determine for themselves who they wanted to associate with.

We should give up our pretence of governing Papua, and put all of New Guinea under the United Nations, administered jointly by us and the Dutch. That way we can be hopeful that these fine natives can eventually march to their own nationhood.

Letters, R Robson. Australia, at this stage, will have to ask herself why, since 1942, she has sacrificed 9,000 of her Servicemen in New Guinea, and why, since 1946, she has spent no less than 98 million Pounds there as a gift. If she did that with security in mind (which of course she did), then she cannot agree with any plan by the Dutch to allow West New Guinea to be occupied by the Indonesians.

Letter, J Wilson, University of Sydney. Tell me, is our possession of any part of New Guinea essential to our security? What may have been true in 1941-5 may no longer be so.

If it is not indispensable, if it is even viewed as a potential liability, why jeopardise our relations with our neighbours whose goodwill may be important, and may be worth more than defending the status quo for reasons that are no longer important to us.

Letters, C Usher. It is folly to talk about imposing our will on two other sovereign countries, and telling them what to do with territory they have a valid claim to. In the long run, if they do not bow to our wishes, what are we going to do? Can we blockade Indonesia and Holland? Surely not. Can we attack or invade them? Don't be silly. Could we tell on them to the UN? A fat lot of good that would do. We cannot do a think except to get these two friendly nations offside.

So I suggest that we learn to make friends with them, and that way we might be able to influence them.

Letters, H McMillan. I must congratulate you on your outspoken criticism of the shameful sell-out to the

Indonesian Government. In our first major diplomatic clash with the East, we have been found hopelessly inept, and have given Subandrio a bloodless victory. We surely let our Dutch friends down, and have paved the way for many troubles in the future.

Letters, Kevin Starr. Indonesia came to independence by a harder road than Australia did. She is struggling to maintain the authority of her Government and needs help to do so. She has no British Empire to stand by her as Australia had in the early days.

An unstable and unfriendly Government could, indeed, be a threat to Australia's security, but a strong and independent Indonesia would be a defence against aggression from our north. Both Britain and the US Governments have recognised this by supplying substantial quantities of arms to Indonesia, to help the Government maintain order, and as a counter to supplies and offers received from Russia. Half of the aid, which Australia gives to maintain Malaya's security, would if given to Indonesia, make her our firm friend.

If we inject a little commonsense (and geography) into the present anti-Indonesia hysteria, we will see that Indonesian Timor is almost as close to Australia as is West New Guinea. Therefore, any danger to Australia's security has been there for 14 years or so. Most schoolchildren are aware of this, but the defence "experts" haven't noticed it up to now.

Placed as we are geographically, it is surely obvious that, without Asian goodwill, **Australia has no long-range future as a white continent**. A thousand million Asians just can't be wrong.

Letters, Bertram Ford. The Herald has to be congratulated on its stand against what can fairly be described as the Federal Government's sell-out on

New Guinea; no Minister or Cabinet has any right to bind this country on such a matter without consulting Parliament, especially as the Ministerial agreement is a complete reversal of its established policy, and no hint was given during the election campaign.

It is Parliament's duty to reject this unauthorised agreement and to insist on a new deal. Otherwise, Australia will be held in contempt.

Letters, D Buchanan. The Government's shock **tergiversation** over the West New Guinea issue re-classifies the policy of Minister Casey from the puerile to dangerously inept. For those who regard a common frontier with an unstable Asiatic power as disconcerting, it is to be hoped that in the interest of our national security the Dutch refuse to move out.

If the Dutch now call us "perfidious Australia", then blame the Minister for External Affairs.

Letters, RETURNED AIRMAN. No part of New Guinea must ever be handed over to an Asian power. Concede that territory now and say goodbye to our security tomorrow. The Communists are securing bases all over the world. West New Guinea might be one.

Do you concede that Menzies and Casey can defy the will of the people as a whole? The people are opposed to this tragic blunder. Why cannot we revoke this decision? These men cannot sell out our community's security and the Papuans' freedom as they like.

Another Billy Hughes is needed. He put his country first, stood his ground and fought a manly fight, no matter what the odds.

Letters, E Ellis. Adolescent Australia has now embarked for the first time on a decision of her own in the face of an awakening Asia; she is laying the first stone of her future foreign relations. Let us hope that those who are in full possession of the facts will not only protect our interests but also establish goodwill. As an individual nation we have not the power to force Indonesia from her prize. As a member of the bloc of Western nations our strategic advantage in securing west New Guinea would be more than offset by adverse and united Asian opinion fostered by Communist China.

Comment. You can see how deeply the community was divided on the issue. It took a long time, measured in decades, before the bulk of Australians lost their uneasiness about Indonesia. Indeed, there is a reasonable number of citizens who are still not quite sure.

From my own point of view, I look back on the fifty years since this episode, and reflect that, despite a number of hot issues that have come between our two nations at times, our relationship with Indonesia has remained pretty good. In fact, when you consider just how big the differences are between us in so many ways, and also how closely we live to each other, I think the level of harmony has been, and is, remarkable.

POULTRY NEWS

Professor T Robinson, from Animal Husbandry, at the University of Sydney, told a conference of poultry growers today that they needed to glamorise their products. He urged that eggs be promoted from the breakfast table to the luncheon and dinner table. Fried eggs should go hand in hand not only with the breakfast bacon, but the evening steak and sausages and chops and kidneys. As for poultry meat, it must be brought out of the luxury class, and placed on every table, **not twice a year**, but once a week.

Comment. Professor Robinson was right. For me, poultry was on the table twice a year, at Easter and Christmas. Then, out would come the tomahawk, and the hunt for the lucky sacrifice was on in the chook-pen. This particular bird had been warned a dozen times that she was the chosen one, but still she flapped her trimmed wings and squawked and fluttered along with her mates in some display of unbecoming petulance.

Her head then was doomed to fall. If you have ever tried to get a chook to lie still and get its head cut off, you will know that they are usually not at all co-operative. Once I tried to use hypnosis by drawing a line on the ground outwards in front of her eyes. It did not work at all on the chook, though my new hypnotised young wife lay down and did not move for two days. Anyway, after a few near misses, and the occasional snick, the blood spurted, and the chook was ready for hanging from the Hills Hoist to let the blood and mucus run out.

Then the metal bathtub, no longer in regular use because of running hot water, would appear, and the chook would take a dive into the steam. Feathers would be plucked, half-feather by half-feather, until the bird, now quite naked, was ready for gutting. This was a simple process. Simply get the sharp kitchen knife, stick it under its rib cage, and drag it slowly and with great difficulty towards its bottom. The intestines and giblets, and heart and liver and lungs, together with half-digested food and stomach lice and worms, would all spill out over your bare feet, and make a terrible stench. But that is too horrible to even speak about, so I will spare you mention of it.

Then the carcase would be chilled. No longer was the ice box good enough for that. Nor was the old gas refrigerator. Nowadays we had an electric fridge, with a light that came on when we opened the door. And which was said to go off when the door was shut. Many of us did not believe this, but the device was too small to let us test it out. But back to the bird. It was now over to the cook, and then the carver, and then the eaters.

The poultry meat tasted great, and was indeed a luxury to us. The whole bi-annual romp was worth the effort, though I doubt whether I would have been prepared to make it a tri-annual event. Professor Robinson and his growers obviously knew of the processing changes that had to occur, and so there is the abundance of chicken in shops today. But let me add that last Christmas I was on a small farm where the tomahawk mode of slaying and processing was still in vogue, and the bird then tasted just as it had fifty tears earlier, and much, much better than my current supermarket chicks.

INNOVATIONS

Three important developments were about to make themselves felt in society.

A new service has been created that allows people to ring a number and receive **a current weather forecast.** A woman's voice will be recorded at two hour intervals, from 6am to 10 pm, that will give details of weather expectations. This is a new service to be provided by the P.M.G. and the Weather Bureau.

Then there is the giant leap forward of being able to **place newspaper ads by phone.**

Mr Conrad Hilton, a well-known American millionaire, predicted that money would be almost obsolete in 15 years. Its place would be taken by **credit cards.** "Buy now and pay later" will be the motto. Cards will be used for every type of goods and service.

Comment. Rubbish. Credit cards will never work.

NEWS AND VIEWS

Letters, TOURIST. I was interested in your recent article on the shortage of bath plugs in rural areas. Quite recently I was travelling in the western districts in an organised motor tour and found not only bath plugs missing, but in some western towns no water or wash basins in the rooms and a lack of supervision generally in some country hotels.

Letters, O Bisset. A recent Gallup Poll said that 85 per cent of those interviewed thought that hire-purchase charges were too high. It would be interesting now to take a poll on the following equally bald questions. Are eggs too dear? Are fares too high? Is the cost of government too high? Is land too dear? Are wages too low? If the affirmative replies to these questions do not exceed 85 per cent, I will gladly donate 10 Pounds to a superannuation fund for Gallop Poll experts.

One wonders is there any value in this sort of Poll.

Letters, G Lucas. On a number of occasions lately after watching TV, I have felt a strong desire to drink a certain widely advertised beer. As a lifelong tea-totaller, I find this difficult to understand and can only assume that some experimentation is taking place in regard to **subliminal** perception advertising, which has already been banned in the UK, and is under close examination in the USA.

If so, what can a citizen do to put an end to this intolerable invasion of intellectual privacy?

MARCH: BILLY IS STILL HERE

In Melbourne, he had presented to large audiences for a full month, and thought quite rightly that he had earned a rest. His Sydney stint was not due to start until April 12, so during March he prepared his material for next month, and also had a swim or two up on the Gold Coast in Queensland. Meanwhile, his entourage was getting ready for Sydney. Charles Rigg, Director of Counseling, said that more than 8,000 counselors had been recruited for Sydney. This was the largest number the campaign had ever recruited, the next largest number had been in Toronto, Canada, and the number there was 1,600.

Counseling training sessions were offered in six venues around Sydney, in the evenings after work. There were eight sessions of training at each location weekly, and successful councellors were required to attend at least seven of these sessions. For example, 2,000 persons attended the 5.30 training at the Town Hall every Monday for eight weeks. Then, 1,500 came for the 8.30 session. Hurstville had 1,600, while Parramatta got 1,700. Many more were turned away because there were no facilities for them. Mr Rigg said that the response had been unprecedented, and that the recruits were keener than anywhere else in the world. He said that they were taking their instruction "like a glass of cool water."

WHAT HAPPENED TO OUR TEA?

This wide brown land was still one where tea-drinkers predominated. Coffee was on the way in but still remained fairly exotic, and the ladies from across the road were still likely to drop in for a cuppa. But something terrible was happening.

Letters, J Wood. May I voice a protest against the quality of so-called tea that is foisted on the tea-drinking public nowadays. The contents of the tea packets seem to be largely composed of a coarse dust, with a generous portion of fine dust added for good measure. Neither in quality, nor in the quantity of tea per pound, can it compare with the pre-war product.

Would some well-informed reader please tell us tea drinkers the reasons for this. Do Australian buyers buy only the poor grades of tea? Is better quality tea available in this country? If so, where and at what price? What "cop" per pound are the tea companies making out of this rich, alluvial dust?

Letters, D Porter. I should like to support Mr Wood. Here, I find that tea, under a multiplicity of trade-names and all sorts of quality grading, are all unpalatable. For years I have watched the papers for some such protest, but apart from one Indian visitor, the public seems to be unaware of the deterioration of the quality of tea offered for sale.

Letters, R. Armitage. This may solve Mr Wood's problem of what is wrong with tea. My wife has tried putting more tea in the pot, changing to different brands, even boiling in a billy. But still it didn't taste like tea.

At last, however, from friends who have just been to Ceylon, where they visited a tea plantation, we found out what may be the reason. Their guide explained that the high-growth tea, light in colour and rich in aroma, is reserved for connoisseurs. The medium growth makes up the bulk of the export. Finally, there is the low growth which forms a brew, dark in colour, but with little flavour. **"Fortunately for us,"** said the guide, **"Australians love it. They buy it all."**

Letters, M Chong. If Australians would stop making tea with boiling water they would get a better cup of tea. The water should be closely watched and as soon as it comes to the boil, the heat should be turned off, the tea pot having been previously heated.

Letters, Lillian Lennie. Mr Wood should be interested to know that my tea dust has in it a staining agent that also stains my cups. We do not even get pure tea dust.

Letters, R Parkinson. In the 12 years I have been in Australia, I have not been able to get good tea. It is all muddy, and not refreshing. A friend in New Zealand sends it to me and it is clean tasting and refreshing.

On one occasion I had just poured a cup of tea without milk when I was interrupted, and when I returned 10 minutes later the tea was bright violet in colour.

Letters, W Hoy. The chemical tests of the Customs Department debar any but reasonable tea from entering the country. One of the tests for caffeine includes the introduction of ammonia water which turns the brew purple or violet. It seems that some of the chemical gas found its way into the tea of Mr Parkinson, and brought about this peculiar and unusual result.

As to "tea as black a coal" as reported in your columns, I would advise anyone who had such to take it to the Health Department for analysis, because tea answering that description has never been grown.

Letters, K Read, Commissioner, the Tea Bureau. The price of tea in Australia was controlled for the fourteen years leading up to 1956. During that period, only one standard of medium-quality tea was imported by the Government for distribution and blending by tea packers. The public became used to paying only one price for its tea. Only since the beginning of 1956 have new high-quality teas at varying higher retail costs become available on this market.

Today, there is a definite choice of quality, and though by no means all grocers stock these good-quality pure Ceylon teas, the demand is growing, and more grocers are responding to that demand rather than lose custom. To those requiring top quality at cheaper cost, I would say that with any commodity the public has to pay a small premium for quality, and tea is no exception.

It is indeed remarkable that good-quality tea is nearly five times cheaper than its nearest rival in the beverage field, namely, coffee.

Comment. There was no mention at this date of tea bags. But tea was not the only commodity under the hammer. Milkshakes and beer, and marmalade jam got the treatment as well.

OTHER HEALTHY DRINKS

Letters, E Campbell. That innocent refreshment, the milkshake, first became popular in the early 1930's. Milk bars proliferated all over our cities just as espresso shops and fruit-juice "spots" do today. They were called "4-penny milk bars", and for that price, one had two full glasses of a creamy, frothing mixture of milk (one-half pint), ice-cream, and any one of a number of flavourings.

Nowadays one usually pays one shilling and one penny for a milkshake, and some curious practices have crept into milkshake-making.

First, the half-pint measure seems to have shrunk to the size of a smallish teacup. Second, the time allowed on the electric mixer has been reduced to a maximum of something like three or four seconds, with the operator keeping a firm hand on it throughout the brief process and snatching it off lest it remain on a fraction too long.

One might swallow this – less milk and less shaking, for treble the price – but we are now being asked to go without ice-cream altogether – or pay extra for it, as though it was not one of the basic ingredients.

A glass of milk costs sixpence. How quixotic of us to pay another seven pence to have less than a glassful mixed with flavouring and served in a metal container, as a rule, instead of a glass.

Letters, J Swift. Mr Campbell, the milkshake authority, is well out on his dates. That innocent beverage was a virile rival to the equally popular corpse-reviver, the threepenny shandy gaff of the very early 1900s.

I mind the time when, around about 1902-3, the glittering milk bar of one Guiseppe Portovino or his successor, in King Street, Newtown, was crowded with lads and lasses seeking solace in the contemplation of a milkshake. Laced with flavouring, after a tour of Saturday night shopping.

The instrument of torture that converted the lactose fluid into a pint or more of milkshake approximated a modern rock-driller. But, brother, it shook.

Letters, Kerwin Magraith. The exciting news that, for the first time, vodka is being included for judging at the Royal Easter Show might move the spirit of Mr Khrushchev, but to a born and bred Australian, who, like most Australians, prefers beer, why is it that the Show does not include this most popular of all alcoholic liquids.

It is truly extraordinary that Sydney does not pit the excellence of its beer against that of the most famous international beers. Might it be that our beer is in fact not so good after all, or is it that the Royal Agricultural Society has not thought of introducing a competition for the best beer offered.

Letters, Gordon Bridges. If tea has deteriorated, then what about the flavoured gelatine posing as marmalade in Sydney today? In hot weather, the gelatine runs away as water. In my travels, I found there is only one true marmalade produced in this State, in a southern town. It is so good that it cannot be brought in Sydney groceries, but I was fortunate enough to arrange for supplies.

PICK ON SOMEONE YOUR OWN SIZE

Tony Maddigan was a very promising boxer, who had won a Gold Medal at the recent Commonwealth Games. With a lot of hype from our local Press, he went to the US for their prestigious Golden Gloves Championship in California with the idea that if he was successful, he would turn professional. Many people here thought he had a brilliant future ahead of him, despite his 29 years of age.

Unfortunately for him, in his first fight he was pitted against a lanky American negro, a seventeen-year-old schoolboy. Maddigan constantly landed severe body blows that made the lad winch, but the young fellow used his long reach to jab and jolt Maddigan's head, and then his superior speed to dance out of range.

The fight went the full distance, of three rounds. Maddigan lost in a disputed points decision. After the fight, he thought that he had had enough and that he would go home and "give the game away." It was something of a sad affair, after the high hopes everyone had for him. His boxing world had collapsed round him, and he was reported to be dejected.

But, in hindsight, his performance that night might not have been **so** bad. Granted, he had been beaten by a lad twelve years his junior. But he had been **just** beaten. But, even further, that gangly schoolboy turned out to be not just **any** young up-and-comer, but a rather special one. In fact, "the greatest fighter ever." His name: **Cassius Clay.**

The fight was watched by a TV audience of 20 million persons, and helped to bring Clay out of obscurity. He will be remembered for his great prowess, but also for his wonderful piece of self-promotion. "I can float like a butterfly, but sting like a bee."

THE GREAT NEEDLEWORK CONTROVERSY

Letters, SEW AND SEW. I would like very much to see a revision of the methods of teaching dressmaking in our High Schools. I daresay the articles and styles still prescribed were "high fashion" for our grandparents but are absolutely out of date now.

My daughter is an average pupil who, over the last three years' course, has produced (along with her classmates) an apron, a very simple skirt and blouse, and a pair of old-style "bloomers", which any normal teenager would rightly refuse to wear. Finally, a huckaback guest towel, elaborately embroidered. Much time is spent in learning drafting and in the assembling of endless tissue-paper garments.

Drafting is not essential for the average sewer. Why cannot girls be taught to make simple garments from purchased paper patterns when there is such a wonderful variety available? This was not so in the days when the High Schools' dressmaking courses were drawn up, but it is time this was taken into consideration.

An adult attending a good dressmaking course can complete a well-fitting simple garment after eight lessons, so surely quick young brains could show even better results. I would prefer my daughter to make her own clothes from purchased patterns rather than spend time on an endless flow of guest towels, embellished with cross-stitch. It is time for these school courses to be modernised and adapted to present needs.

Letters, Eunice Graham. I would like to take issue with SEW AND SEW. I have learned needlework for the whole of five years of my secondary schooling, and feel well qualified to do this.

In the first three years all members of my class learned to use a sewing machine and made some garments, including an apron, a cap for cookery-class, a tray-cloth, several undergarments, a night-dress, a cross-stitch table-centre, a skirt, and several knitted articles. We also learned drafting, and made tissue-paper models and "processes."

SEW AND SEW has the wrong idea if she thinks that time so spent is time wasted, as it teaches the basic principles of garment construction before the student practices on the "real thing" and so saves many costly mistakes. Embroidery and smocking are also taught, and far from being a waste of time are essential in the making of underwear, children's clothes and household linen.

On entering High School I could not even use a sewing machine, but after 12 months' tuition could make some of my clothes, using simple purchased patterns, and at the end of Third Year make all of my own clothes. Two extra years to the Leaving Certificate and I was able to sew even the most difficult designs. This tuition cost my parents only a few pounds but in the eight years since I left school it saved me and my family hundreds.

Far from being out of date, the teaching in our High Schools is modern and practical, and I believe that it should be a compulsory subject for all girls at least up to the Intermediate Certificate standard.

Letters, STITCHES. I am a sincere and interested teacher of needlework who considers that the trouble really starts in the primary classes. Years ago I dared to deviate slightly from the syllabus in allowing one class to make an attractive and useful article rather than the despised one of the syllabus, although the same processes were used as demanded by the regulations. The result was most pleasing, the girls were happy and so was I. Later that year I had an inspection and was told that the despised article was "a must", but I was not given a sensible reason for the "must".

I have not deviated from the narrow path again, but as the years pass I find girls are less interested and myself frustrated and cranky.

INTERNATIONAL AFFAIRS

The spirit of international co-operation that was showing early in the year was still evident. **Here, at home**, we were now positively cosy with the Russians. **Overseas.** Britain's Prime Minister McMillian had enjoyed a pleasant trip to Russia, and was now in the US talking to Richard Nixon, who was Vice President at that stage.

Nikita Khrushchev was talking about visiting America, and his delegates in the UN were being helpful in seeking a solution to the perennial problem of what they should do with their German mandates and the signing of a Peace Treaty with that nation. **It seemed that full-scale peace might break out.** What a shock that would be.

But there were quite a few kill-joys still around. Many people, New Australians in particular, had written to newspapers **complaining about our re-opening of diplomatic relations with Russia**. And a few were frightened by the possibility of opening up trade with China. Then, there was this lady who expressed the disquiet of many others.

Letters, (Miss) P Davis. The announcement that the Menzies Government has agreed to restore diplomatic relations with Soviet Russia underlines a developing trend most instructive to those who voted for Menzies last November believing that their vote would return a Government which, though defective on many issues, would at least take a strong stand on Communism.

Most informed observers believe that Australia must build her population if she is to survive the challenge of Asia. Yet the Menzies Government has quietly reduced our annual migrant intake to the totally inadequate figure of 100,000 or so.

Now, we have "peace" with Russia. Quite obviously, to any trained observer, the Government is preparing the way for recognition of China. It is becoming very difficult to discern any vital difference between the Menzies "anti-Communism" and the Evatt brand, which the electors so decisively rejected last November.

ADVICE FOR WOMEN

Hollywood sex-symbol, Zaa Zaa Gabor was divorced this week. **Again.** After the proceedings were formalised, she told the assembled Press. "Love is of the utmost importance in marriage. Every woman should keep trying until she finds it."

APRIL: RICHARDSON REPORT

For the past few months, a Committee of about half a dozen worthy gentlemen had been meeting at various times to work out how much Federal politicians should get paid. Of course, this august body had been carefully chosen by Prime Minister Menzies, so that its members were certain to make recommendations for good increases in salaries and allowances. There was nothing unusual in that. In the past, parliamentary salaries had generally been reviewed periodically, and the rewards for service were at least in line with the cost of living increases.

In April, this Richardson Committee reported, and this time it excelled all the efforts of previous committees. It suggested that the ordinary backbencher should get a salary increase of about 25 per cent, a typical Minister about 40 per cent, and the Prime Minister was worthy of a 70 per cent upgrade. All of this went hand-in-hand with generous allowances for travel, and stamps and propaganda and increased pensions and perks, so that our representatives would all be very much better off.

The opposition to this was immediate and widespread. Of course, pay rises for politicians are always criticised. That was just as true then as it is now. But these proposed rises came at a time when every politician, from Menzies down, had been lecturing the nation on the need for wage restraint. From their mouths, their was nothing but scorn for those workers and Unions who were betraying the nation's interests and seeking wage increases at a time when inflation was the big political bogey of the day. But the big question was, would the politicians accept this generosity?

Or would they forgo it for something smaller, or perhaps for nothing at all

There was no doubt in the minds of the population. The newspapers were quite sure that the politicians would take their increased pay, and the readers of those newspapers absolutely flooded them with critical comments. In fact, the Sydney Morning Herald later stated that this subject had encouraged more Letters than any other subject since the War.

> **Letters, D White.** Never has public indignation been so unanimous and bitter as over the proposed Federal members' salary increases, yet the average elector helplessly asks what can be done about it. My answer is that as one cannot use the ballot-box, try the postal-box and write to one's local member.
>
> It is too much to expect that the salary increases will be rejected, but if a member receives thousands of letters in opposition to them, he might think twice before voting for the obnoxious hand-out. He might at least amend it, thus saving much wasteful public money.
>
> **Letters, S Yankowsky.** There is something odious in the unanimity of the Ministers as well as in the expected unanimity of the M.P.s in voicing their assent to the Richardson Committee. Surely, the M.P.s must have the confidence of their constituents, and so must Parliament as a whole have the confidence of the nation.
>
> There is, however, one point of extreme importance to be noted. Apart from political trust, apart from the fact that they are our spokesmen in questions of policy, it is essential that our representatives in the Parliament should be, as individuals, men of high prestige, absolute integrity and moral excellence.

Accepting a high public office always entails high moral obligations, and the services freely undertaken by men in exalted positions are everywhere in the world regarded as an honour, not a source of monetary gain and an ordeal to complain of.

Contrary to the British parliamentary tradition, the Richardson Committee has utterly ignored this consideration in its cynical document. **Presenting Parliamentarians, with their present-day salary plus allowances, as paupers unable to pay their expenses, deprived of their leisure and security, suffering through disruption of family life, separated from their wives and children, as victims of imaginary tribulations and a target for abuse and misrepresentation, is more than one can bear.**

Comment. What a beautiful long, correct, sentence.

Letters, D F Keegan. Permit me to touch on two aspects of the 1959 political Easter egg, namely the composition of the body that laid it and a comparison with politicians' remuneration in England.

The Prime Minister naturally turned again to the same Melbourne businessmen who had handed it out to the Canberra boys on a previous occasion. But if he had been a little more astute he would surely have called in one or more High Court Judges. Then, if their decision had been favourable, it would at least have given these fantastic rises some semblance of judicial respectability. Not many people will agree that the wealthy head of a chain store is the proper arbiter of a politician's remuneration.

My son is a conservative MP at Westminster. His attendances there average four times those of our MPs. Whereas his Australian counterpart finds it perfectly feasible to live 500 or more miles from the House my son, who lived in his own constituency of

Nottingham, has recently been compelled to move to a new residence just outside London so as to be able to carry out his political obligations.

In England, it really is a full-time job but when I compare salaries plus "perks" in the two countries I find that for four times as much work my son will receive just about 50 per cent of Australian members' takings. Finally, when the staggering etceteras are added to Mr. Menzies' salary, we find that he is much higher paid than the Commonwealth's senior politician, the Prime Minister of England.

Basic wage rise. The list of criticisms went on and on. One argument was that the salaries would not need adjustment if it was not for inflation. And who, it was asked, was responsible for inflation? Another argument was that public companies needed a vote from shareholders to ratify changes to the salaries of Board members. Surely, this should also be true for the biggest "company" in the nation. A Mr Lesslie, from Roseville, thought:

> Among politicians surely there should be the feeling that the job is worth doing, leading to the satisfaction of a job well done. The worthwhile achievements in Australia's history, and those which are still continuing today in all fields of research and exploration, have not resulted from great pay cheques, but from men of vision with thoughts for the great future of this country.

The job of selling the pay deal to the public was made harder by an Arbitration Court's decision to increase the NSW Basic Wage by a shilling for the March quarter. Here is an eloquent comment on this.

Letter, K Roddy. Whacko. I am to get one extra shilling a week in my pay packet. I do not have to do extra work for that money. I get it just for doing what I have been doing. It sounds like a good deal to me.

But, let me compare it to other increases. Our Federal politician back-benchers will get an increase of 1,000 pounds per year. That works out at 20 Pounds per week. Or to put it in the currency I am familiar with, 400 shillings per week. That is, an **increase** of 400 shillings per week. Just for doing what they did before.

Let me think about that. My increase is one shilling. Their increases are 400 shillings. I work in a pit and shovel coal 40 hours per week under stinking conditions. They do not do that.

I think I am in the wrong job.

There were some supporters for the increases. One writer argued that it was three years since a salary increase, and that by simple arithmetic there should be an increase of at least 12 per cent to allow for inflation. Others said that the duties and responsibilities were so great that parliamentarians deserved a higher salary, simply because of the work that they did. Still others said that it was silly to expect representatives to work for less than they could get elsewhere, because such people do not have the judgement that their job demanded. Several writers said that the amount of abuse that they and their families had to suffer justified an even greater increase.

But the vast majority of writers were emphatic. The salary increase was seen, by most of the public, to be over the top. However, from this point the inevitable occurred. Some of the Labor members said they would vote against the proposal when it came to Parliament. But when the chips were down, they voted for the increases because of "party solidarity." The President of the Federal Labor Party, Joe

Chamberlain, was so affronted by the Party's proposed pro-increase stance that he resigned in a very grand flourish. But two weeks later, he was back in the job. In the States, **all** parliamentarians were emphatically against it, but a few months later, as their own States proposed flow-on increases, they changed their tunes, and supported the changes, on the basis that they were then necessary so as to "maintain relativities." Menzies, and the Liberals, were quite straight-forward. They were all **for** the proposed Bill. So, after another month of huffing and puffing, the changes were passed by both Houses.

Comment. At that time I was teaching maths in a large High School in Sydney. It was a Catholic school, with a minimum of forty boys per class, and forty periods of face-to-face teaching each week. In short, I was doing an honest day's work. My salary then was 1,600 Pounds per year. The new salary for a backbencher was 2,700 Pounds. How did that compare?

Certainly MPs worked longer hours than I did, and they were on call at all hours of the day and night, and they got a lot of snide remarks and abuse from the nitwits in the community. I also got 10 weeks holidays per year. When you weigh up **all** the factors, MPs were worth more, but not too much more. Based only on my salary versus theirs, I think Richardson got it about right. I would not have wanted them to get less, and indeed I would have wondered about their ability to make sound judgements if they had been prepared to work for less.

So there the matter rested. Since then, about every three years, soon after a new Parliament is elected, a remuneration committee is empowered to make recommendations on the salaries and benefits of Members, and it comes in with proposals that keep the new salaries well above the average wages of the community, but not too far above. There is always vocal opposition from the public, but nothing like that over the Richardson report. **It seems to me** that people have gradually come to the conclusion that the MPs are actually here to stay, and that if they want them to be of a reasonable standard, they will have to be paid reasonable wages.

IMBECILE CHILDREN

A staff journalist, employed by the Sydney Morning Herald, (SMH) wrote in mid-April of the problems associated with looking after deformed and imbecile children. The following Letter replied in a somewhat garbled way to this article, and brought forth a number of sad responses.

Letters, Sandra Musgrave. Your correspondent's article "What do we do with imbecile children?" raises a subject which cannot be ignored, and I am one of many who feel that the law should be altered. There are thousands of normal healthy children who would be only too grateful for a home and a mother's love, yet must live in homes while these unhappy deformed creatures are receiving a mother's love and can offer neither appreciation nor companionship in return.

It is understandable that a mother, having borne the child, would be reluctant to part with it. But would it not be better to have the child destroyed before she became too attached to it, and shower her motherly love on an adopted child. This way she has saved her own child from an unhappy abnormal life.

Letters, R Davidson, M.D., B.S. If left to nature, these deformed children would quickly die from inanition, illness or accident. It does appear on the surface that euthanasia in such cases would not only be a sensible and humane solution but that it could be, in the future, a necessity as the number of afflicted increases and the institutions become filled to overflowing.

It would be hard to get laws to do this. Firstly, because a correct diagnosis in the early months of life could be fallacious. Secondly, among the parents, there will be a very small percentage who will ever agree to their child being permanently taken from them. They will carry on with hope for improvement ever present in their hearts.

The answer to this problem is for the public to see that their governments provide very adequate financial aid for the building, extension and improvements of mental institutions and to make them so efficient and attractive as will encourage parents to place their severely afflicted children in these homes to enable them to carry on with further family building without the extra burdens and strain that such unfortunate children bring.

Parents who resort to euthanasia can never be satisfied that they acted correctly.

Letters, R Morgan. Surely the majority of us will agree that to keep alive grotesquely deformed or imbecile beings is, in fact, a form of cruelty to the parents, the child itself and the community at large.

I have complete respect for the doctrines of the Church and for the Hippocratic Oath, but if we can rationalise in the case of war and self-sacrifice by saying that God sanctions murder and suicide, surely we can apply the same reasoning to infanticide in special cases, which action serves the same, if not a better service to the world.

Letters, PERPLEXED. As the mother of a Mongoloid baby born also with a hole in the heart, could someone tell me why that baby's life was actually fought for by the staff of a large city hospital?

The baby would not suck and for three months was kept alive by feeding through a tube. The mental agony that she and three other normal children went through I do not wish to recall.

After three months she began to suck and I brought her home where she died three months later. I was advised that this would very likely happen. Was the struggle for her life worthwhile in any way?

Comment. These were the first four of about a dozen Letters concerning deformed infants. I found all of the correspondents surprisingly matter of fact, and guessed they had long passed the stage of agonising over the morality of infanticide. I, on the other hand, have never been in contact with it at all. So, I pondered for a while about religious objections, and the "thou shalt not kill" philosophy. And about the right to life and other ethical questions, and also the concept of limited resources being spent on hopeless cases. The more I thought about it, the more I realised what an impossibly difficult question this is.

If the infant is allowed to live, the parents, and families, faced with such situations, have to live with it 24 hours a day, seven days a week, for perhaps years or longer. I can understand them becoming completely matter of fact, and just wanting some relief from somewhere. For those who choose to terminate a life, there would be few of us who could walk away without feelings of guilt, and the nagging worry about whether some miracle cure might have saved the situation. Nowadays discussions on euthanasia tend to revolve around the elderly, and infanticide seems to be off the public agenda. And nowadays, with improvements in medical diagnosis, some damaged foetuses are aborted before birth. But this is **still**, inevitably, **an issue**, a forgotten one. All I can say is my heart goes out to all those who are forced to make the difficult decisions and then live with them.

THE FUTURE OF THE GLOBE

Two well-known and prominent figures this week made grave pronouncements on the future of the earth. They, quite independently of each other, predicted that the world was unlikely to survive for very much longer.

Well-known playwright, Tennessee Williams, scorned talk about what type of car a person might own in ten years time. His view is that "none of us will be here by then. The hot breath of disaster and destruction is already on the backs of our necks."

With a similar view, Sir Robert Watson-Watt, known as the "Father of Radar", believes that mankind will destroy itself with "either hydrogen bombs, deadly toxins or nerve gases. Or more likely, once we get started, the combination of all three will finish us off before we know it."

CITIZEN'S ARREST

The report below is for the Rugby League fans.

Rugby League second-row forward for Manly and for Australia, was sent off the field today in a match against Eastern Suburbs at the Sports Ground. Mossop was involved in a scuffle with East's forward, Ron Potter, and the referee adjudged that Mossop had used an elbow. The referee had spoken twice before to Mossop about pugnacious tendencies, and this time he ejected him from the play. Mossop was also sent off last season in a match against England at the Sydney Cricket ground. He will appear before the Judiciary tomorrow night, charged with elbowing Potter in the face.

Comment. At the hearing, he was relieved to receive only a caution.

Mossop, always a favourite with the crowds, was a flamboyant, handsome man, not conspicuous for his conformity. A few years later, when he retired as a player, **he became a TV personality by moving into Rugby League commentary**, calling hundreds of games. His forceful comments won him many friends, and perhaps lost him a few as well.

After he retired from calling, he once hit the news in an **incident that involved nude bathers** who were using a beach near his house. He could not get the bathers to move off the beach, so he made citizen's arrests of the trespassers, and held them there until the police arrived. There was a lot of comment about this.

NEWS AND VIEWS

High Court of Australia, April 21st. The Full Court today ruled that **certain provisions** of the Commonwealth Re-Establishment and Employment Act **were now invalid**.

Under this Act, **preference in employment and housing had been given to ex-Servicemen from World War II**. That is, if two persons of equal merit applied for a job, and one of them was an ex-Serviceman and the other was not, then **the position went automatically to the former**. Likewise if both men were seeking to rent the same premises.

The prevailing opinion of the seven judges was that such matters now belonged in the realm of employment, and to claim that they were still a matter of Defence was spurious. Given the passage of time since the War, the Defence argument was impossible to sustain.

Comment. This provisions of the Act were now gone, and everyone was on an equal footing.

News Item, Tibet April 3ʳᵈ. Chinese forces are continuing to pour across the border into Tibet, and the meagre forces of Tibet are no match for them. The Chinese have already occupied the capital, and have complete control of the city. The Dalai Lama has gone into hiding and it is believed that he will find sanctuary in India.

Comment. About sixty years later, this same Dalai Lama is basically still on the run from Chinese forces. The Chinese occupation has been good for the modernisation of Tibet, but it remains a moot point whether this has been good or bad for the nation.

MAY: NEW GUINEA NATIVES

In mid-May, a New Guinea farmer was brought before the Supreme Court for killing a native who worked for him on a plantation. The native had been struck a few blows, and one of these had ruptured his spleen, and he had died soon after the attack. The Judge, Mr Justice Kelly, who sat on the case, decided that, while it was obvious that the death occurred as a result of the incident, the farmer was guilty of an offence "less than murder." He levied a fine of 150 Pounds.

In handing down his judgement, he explained that if he had gaoled Seer, the farmer, he would have been compelled by law to impose a sentence of six months or more. If he had done that, the sentence would, again by law, have to be served in Australia. That meant that when Seer was released, and applied for re-entry to the Territory of New Guinea, his application would have been automatically refused because he had served a major gaol term. Keeping in mind that some New Guinea natives had congenitally weak spleens, he thought it proper not to gaol the farmer, because that course of action would remove him permanently from his family and farm.

This decision was widely criticised in Australia. Twenty two Trade Unions wrote to the Minister for the Territories, Mr Paul Hasluck, and described it as a scandalous state of affairs, and forecast that the shameful discrimination by law in New Guinea would cause irrevocable harm among our own New Guinea and Papuan peoples, and among the neighbouring peoples of South-East Asia. Professor Stout, head of the Department of Philosophy at Sydney

University, said "I was shocked at the penalty for killing a man, and shocked at the implication that the hitting of natives in New Guinea was an everyday thing. If they are always hitting natives in New Guinea, then it is time they stopped it."

Correspondence to the newspapers was voluminous. It brought forth many divergent views on affairs in New Guinea, and the attitudes then towards the natives. It made **this** elderly, white, middle-class male, living smugly in suburbia, sit up and take notice.

Letters, I Henson. Since 1941, almost every item of news about New Guinea has been distressing. For example, the frequent armed conflict between natives and Government patrols, and the tragic attempt to collect taxes through the agency of three white officers and eighty armed native constables. This job was previously done by one white officer with one unarmed native constable to act as orderly. Then there are frequent stories of labour unrest. And now the extraordinary judgement passed by Judge Kelly.

These and other incidents suggest that the old sad story of Australian aborigines is being re-enacted in New Guinea. Ostensibly, Australian taxpayers are paying 12 million Pounds annually to make New Guinea a defensive rampart against our potential enemies. But, in the process, though facilities are being created that may help our investors to greater profits, the greatest and essential asset of native co-operation is being thrown to the winds.

If we want to get that co-operation, then the local government must be headed, not by a Canberra politician like Mr Hasluck, but by a man thoroughly experienced in native character and mentality; a man of education and intellect who, living in the community, is prepared to devote his life and all his powers to the advancement of Papua-New Guinea and its indigenous inhabitants, and thus to the great and permanent advantage of Australia.

Letters, R Walters. What is of far greater consequence than the unfortunate death of one man is the widespread ill-treatment of natives, which is apparently accepted and condoned by all the Australians living there. That country is strategically of very great importance to Australia, and it seems a pity that the affections of its inhabitants should be alienated in this manner. After a few decades, Papuans will be governing themselves, and it will be infinitely preferable to find a friend on our doorstep.

Letters, R Robson. A large number of New Guinea natives who suffer from malaria develop enlarged spleens. There is **nothing to show** that a man is suffering from this abnormality. Quite a light blow will rupture the spleen and cause death. Natives frequently get a ruptured spleen when fighting or playing games, or carrying on their village activities.

It is unlawful for a European, employer or otherwise, to strike a native. But the great majority of these natives are primitive people who have been accustomed all their lives to the rule of force. Unless the European is prepared to administer light corporal punishment immediately the occasion calls for it, he can never maintain discipline and hold respect among the natives for whom he is responsible. The critics may howl until the Red Kingdom comes, but that has always been the rule in New Guinea, and always will be, and every European who really understands NG subscribes to it.

The Judges there, and not the politicians and Administration officials, are the real guardians of life, law and liberty in the Territory, and that is a fact of major importance. The Territory judges are today men of the utmost probity, held in the highest regard by every class, natives included. They are not responsible to either the Administration or the politicians. They receive their commission directly from the Governor General of Australia.

This means that all you smug, white, middle-class suburbanites should keep your opinions to yourselves. When **you** get the perfect society, then you can come and lecture us. Till that time, leave our judges and courts alone.

Letters, W R Geddes, Professor of Social Anthropology, University of Sydney. One may well wonder from his letter who is the more primitive, Mr Robson and the type of European employer in New Guinea whom he defends, or the native people who in his view require "light corporal punishment."

Certainly his letter shows a lamentable ignorance both of the conditions of native social life on the one hand, and the codes of conduct in most other similar Pacific areas on the other.

In the territories under British Colonial Administration the striking of natives is rare and never condoned. In the independent areas of South-East Asia, Europeans would no longer dare to indulge in it.

It is noticeable that Mr Robson's arrogance extends not only to the natives of New Guinea but apparently also to the Administration and the Government of Australia. The belief held by himself and those whom he supports seems to be that what they do in New Guinea is their own business. But two things must be said here. In the first place, Australia accepted New Guinea trusteeship from the United Nations and the responsibility for conduct belongs to everyone in the Commonwealth. Secondly, the penalty for encouraging racial hatreds, which can mature in a remarkably short time, will fall just as heavily upon the ordinary people of Australia as upon those few persons who can count it as their just desserts.

Finally, let us hear no more of this nonsense about enlarged spleens. If it is so well known in New Guinea that the striking of people is likely to rupture their spleens and kill them, how much more irresponsible the striking of them becomes.

Letters, Edward P Glover, Port Moresby. On the face of it, and on the evidence Australians had before them, there appeared cause for indignation. But this evidence consisted solely of grossly inadequate newspaper reports which had highlighted the trial Judge's unfortunate remarks that accused "had only done what others had done." This comment was taken out of context. In his summing up the Judge was talking about the days **before** the War. He made another remark that the newspapers didn't pick up. He told the farmer that "the good old days are over."

However, if the Judge was somewhat indiscriminate in his choice of words, equally indiscriminate is the criticism by Professor Stout, your correspondents and the 22 Unions who have created this controversy without having any knowledge of the facts or of conditions in New Guinea. Your readers can rest assured that Australians in New Guinea are not bashers, though some may have been in "the good old days." And in the good old days – indeed, in these days – many more whites have died at the hands of blacks than the reverse.

New Guinea natives, even the most primitive in the most isolated places, enjoy the fullest protection of the law. Planters who handle large and often unruly labour forces these days take the law into their own hands at their peril. Use of force to stop plantation brawls has led the planter to court too often. Today the planter leaves the natives to fight it out, often with much bloodshed the result.

Letters, W C Hall, Kelaus Plantation, Madang, New Guinea. The criticisms that have been made have obviously originated from sources that are ill-informed, malicious and to say the least, hysterical. In the eyes of every native in New Guinea, the punishment, that Mr Justice Kelly saw fit to mete out, was fair, just and exactly what every native would expect.

It would appear that the trade-unions and Church leaders who have complained so bitterly, have lost sight of the fact that the European concerned was not on trial for murder, and although he was the cause of the death of the native had not the slightest intention of causing his death.

Do these ill-informed and myopic bodies know that any self-government that may be given to New Guinea, or any other native race, will be only temporary, and will be a green light for that **eventual Asiatic absorption** that only a miracle can forestall?

A POST SCRIPT ON MONGOLISM

Last month we looked at some disturbing aspects of infanticide. Now, as a Post Script, we have another related Letter that talks about aspects of Mongolism.

Letters, R Edwards. As the sister of a subnormal (a mongoloid type), I feel entitled to write you. Other writers have mentioned life times of misery and suffering from working with such children.

Mongolism is definitely not hereditary (it can happen to any woman, possibly, a very young one or particularly one closely approaching the menopause), yet my in-laws objected to my marriage to their son on the grounds on "insanity" in my family. Although we married in spite of this, it caused untold misery and suffering both at the time and when I later became pregnant.

I wonder how many brothers and sisters of mongoloids are similarly affected. Perhaps the brothers and sisters are even more affected than the unfortunate parent, as apart from frequently having to care from them when the parents pass on, the emotional effect of growing up with them is incalculable.

As your correspondents suggest, they should always be diagnosed at birth. I understand that there are definite indications even then. It should also be compulsory for every doctor to immediately inform the parents, who frequently have no idea of what is involved, just what is wrong, what is ahead of them and advise them to act now before they have grown protectively and passionately attached to their child.

I have heard of cases where parents are not informed of the nature of the "backwardness" for many months, of other parents who won't believe it when they are told and even of "kind" doctors who could not bring themselves to tell a loving, anxious mother the terrible news.

Only someone who has had a mongoloid in the immediate family really knows the heartbreak, the continual worry, the social ostracism and the incredible amount of patience called for in rearing them. I am convinced that **euthanasia is the only humane approach to this problem**, with all the proper safeguards, of course, and with the parents' wishes if there are no other children nor ever likely to be.

Euthanasia is a harsh word, but the wrecked lives dedicated to a hopeless lifelong task are definitely harder.

PROBLEMS FOR SOME MIGRANTS

Migrants from overseas continued to pour into Australia. About 120,000 persons in 1958 made the very frightening decision to start a new life on the other side of the globe. The transition was difficult enough for migrants from Britain, but for Europeans the change was severe.

On April 14th the Secretary of the New Australia Council of Labour, highlighted the difficulties. He said that thousands of married migrant women in Australia never go out with their husbands, never meet Australians, see only immediate neighbours of the same nationality, and buy goods from shopkeepers speaking their language. Many of them had never seen a film in Australia. It was not so hard for the men, because they went off to work and picked up some English language there, but the women did not do this.

He lamented that the women were being separated from their children by a language barrier. The children learned at school, and quickly they were talking like Australians with no accent. But not so the mothers. He went on to say it was wrong for migrants to lose their own customs and culture, and that some Australians wanted them to do that. But, he concluded, if that happened it would be a loss for Australia, and would be a negative contribution to our way of life

Comment. This had been a real problem ever since the first War-brides arrived. It was made worse now by the large number of Europeans. There never was an organised solution to it, and that is why it is easy to find small pools of European women in the suburbs who have lived here for fifty years who still have no real grasp of the English language.

ANIMAL TALK

No, this is not cricket news. Seventeen **ducks** from the Highlands of New Guinea will soon arrive in Sydney, and then be transported to Gloucestershire in England where they will be guests of the Wild Fowl Trust. The birds are little, aggressive birds, called Salvadoris, and will be presented to the Duke of Edinburgh, who will accept them on behalf of the Trust and philanthropist, Sir Edward Hallstrom.

He said last night that "none of these ducks have been kept in captivity before. Previous efforts have failed because the persons did not know how to feed them. They are fed on cut tripe, meat, tadpoles and ordinary duck pellets. They are very small, but they eat an awful lot of tripe"

The birds are extremely rare, and are worth about 500 Pounds a pair. Only two or three birds come from each mating. The ducks are now in Bululo, in New Guinea, in the care of the curator of the Trust, Mr T Johnson. He flew out from England so that he might escort them personally by plane to London.

Philippines, Manila. An **Australian emu** died this week at the Manila zoo under suspicious circumstances. It was found in its cage with a deep puncture wound that caused death. The lethal object was a sharp nail protruding from the wall of the cage.

The local Press are talking about the zoo's incompetence and foolishness. The zoo officials, anxious to avoid further criticism, were suggesting that hooligans climbed into the cage, and forced the emu onto the nail. Their latest theory is that the emu deliberately threw itself onto the nail, because it was homesick for Australia. This has raised the question, now being hotly debated, of whether animals will commit suicide. The dominant theory is that it is only man that will do that, but there are substantial numbers who say animals will do so as well.

Press reports. The lucky ones. Two female **rhesus monkeys** were today recovered in the Atlantic Ocean after surviving a pioneer flight into space. Ninety minutes earlier they had been packed into tiny cabins in the nose-cone of an American Jupiter missile, and hurled 300 miles into space. One of the aims of the trial was to determine how much they would be affected by weightlessness. They were in that state for about nine minutes. The monkeys were named Abel and Baker. Abel had a light flashing in front of her, and she was trained to push a button each time the light flashed. These flashes were then transmitted to earth for analysis, presumably to provide employment for a dozen scientists. However, she stopped tapping at the very start of the flight, and so information from this source remains scarce. The eggs and sperm of sea urchins were included in the cargo to evaluate the effects of acceleration, deceleration, weightlessness and radiation. This information will prove to be most useful, given the large number of mating sea urchins who will later make similar flights. **Abel and Baker were the first two creatures to survive the journey from earth into outer space.**

The not-so-lucky. The US, thus encouraged, went one step further. This time they placed **four mice** on board a Discoverer III satellite, and sent them into an orbit, with a low point of 140 miles above the earth, and a high point of 480 miles. They were packed into 1,600 pounds of hardware, and were to travel at 48,000 miles per hour.

The mice themselves came from a strain developed in 1933, and were considerably stronger than the average laboratory or field mouse. They were comparable, said the NASA School of Aviation Medicine, to healthy young men in their twenties. It was expected that their hair would gradually turn white from the progressive effects of radiation. It was not known if their ability to mate with sea urchins would be affected.

The launch of the satellite went well, and for 13 minutes radio messages were received. However, nothing was heard subsequently. Attempts to track it further have not been successful, and it appears that this mission would be classified as a failure. Presumably, the vehicle went out of orbit, and burnt out as it re-entered the atmosphere.

Letters, G Friend. Nowhere in the world does one see as many **lost, starving dogs** as we see in our Sydney streets. The police should have to take them off the streets to a depot. We have depots now for tow-aways. Why not for the dogs, too? Owners can claim them there, or they can be disposed of.

Letters, BIRDWATCHER. It is comforting to learn that scientists are "delighted" that one of their **banded albatrosses** has turned up in the South Atlantic. If it had anything to say on the subject, the bird itself would, one feels, be unlikely to share in this delight. Nor would the innumerable small birds who have been subjected to the attentions of the banders.

An albatross is a very large bird and can doubtless get some of its own back during the banding process. But what of the many nestlings of small birds who are subject to the attentions of the banders each spring, and the unfortunate baby penguins and mutton birds who are dragged from nesting burrows. Many of these are immediately abandoned by their parents and die, some are permanently maimed, and some are caught and die when the bands on their legs foul obstructions. Doubtless very little damage is done in the handling of adult albatrosses even if little is achieved. But indiscriminate and apparently purposeless banding with consequent high mortality rates among nestlings should be stamped out.

The Federal Government should see that the CSIRO does not issue bands at large, but only to experts and for the purpose of named species where it is thought that valuable scientific work can be done. Statistics mean nothing, especially when weighed against the dead nestlings. Banding for bandings sake must be stopped. Otherwise, what in heaven's name, short of moving out to the back country or leaving Australia, must a bird, already menaced by catapults, guns, traps, and predators, do to cope with this new threat to a normal life's enjoyment.

NEWS AND VIEWS

Space travel. In April, the Americans were getting excited because they expected that, within two years, the first men into space would launch forth in the Mercury. The seven astronauts had been chosen for this mission, and were undergoing constant training. In the meantime, the US was gathering as much information as it could about space travel, with varying degrees of luck.

Smoking. Cigarette ads were everywhere. A few early thinkers were just **now** saying that there was a link between smoking and cancer, but most people thought this was far fetched. The body, after all, would filter out harmful agents.

JUNE: WOLFENDEN'S FLOW-ON

In September, 1957, a Committee of 14 members, chaired by John Wolfenden, recommended to the Government of Britain that **acts of homosexuality** in private **should no longer be considered as being criminal** between consenting adults over 21 years of age. The Report generated considerable bitterness and controversy in Britain, and much public re-examination of attitudes to homosexuality. Its philosophy was that "it is not, in our view, the function of the law to intervene in the private lives of citizens, or to seek to enforce any particular pattern of behaviour." General acceptance of the recommendations took a long time to mature, so that the resulting Sexual Offences Act was not passed in Britain until nearly a decade later, in 1967. **Here**, in NSW, a similar Commission had been appointed in 1958, and it would not report for over two years after the British report was released.

In Australia, by 1959, the flow-on from the Wolfenden Act was, however, slowly being noticed. For example, in June 1959, the Sydney Morning Herald, prompted by Wolfenden, presented a serious article on homosexuality, in which it talked about the current state of knowledge about the matter. Other newspapers followed, and below I have presented a summary of what they wrote.

The **general attitude of the community** towards homosexuality was that it did not like it. Some people thought it was "unnatural", and depraved, others looked on it as sinful. Everywhere you went you could find someone prepared to entertain you with the comic impressions of these "punces", with a variety of limp wrists, mincing walks and "hello darling" talk. Beyond these, there were gangs of mindless and witless youths who amused themselves by "poofter bashing" late at night around public lavatories. There were sections of the police force that loitered in known haunts late at night, and posing as poofters, solicited then arrested the miscreants. For any practising homosexual, the atmosphere was hostile and sometimes physically dangerous.

Within families, the whole issue was simply not discussed. It was not talked about in decent families. In some cases, boys were kept away from public lavatories at night, but never knew why. Nor, incidentally, did many of their parents. The whole idea was so foreign to most people, and so few had any idea of it, that homosexuality and paedophilia was not on their agenda, and the thought that clergy could be involved was preposterous. Females, too, were seen as innocent of any taint of this plague that only the most depraved of men were involved with.

Everywhere there was a search going on for the **"causes" of homosexuality.** There were all sorts of reasons for it. **On the medical side,** there were lots of doctors and scientists who aired their opinions. Some of these said emphatically that the "disease" was inherited. These folk sometimes had the idea that if it could be diagnosed early enough, some sort of drug could be found that would cure it for life. Others thought that it had a biological basis that had yet to be defined, but if this basis could be uncovered, then a cure was surely possible. Yet others believed that it was a glandular problem. There were all sorts of "medical" diagnoses, and the one thing they had in common was the idea that a "cure" was a distinct possibility.

Psychologists too were convinced that they had the right slant on it. A surprising number found that the "cause" was to be found in the interactions of homosexuals with their parents. A mother who was too fond and protective of her son. Or a mother who really wanted a girl, and who dressed her boy in girl's clothing. Or a father who was violent towards his son. In such cases, homosexuality could probably be prevented by "ensuring good stable marriages and homes, and in which children are encouraged to mix naturally in the community with both parents who are not over-possessive.".

Some psychologists considered that everyone has a capacity for homosexuality. They thought that for most people the tendency was very brief, even fleeting, and that in most development it passed unnoticed. When the normal sexual development is arrested for some reason, the condition then becomes manifest.

The law was quite clear on the matter. Homosexual acts between males in 1959 were criminal offences, punishable by imprisonment, whether committed in private or in public, with or without consent. Among **the churches**, the Church of England was a standout in the degree of latitude it allowed. It still regarded the homosexual act as sinful, but it thought of the person involved as being in need of skilled help as well as salvation. Other churches were more condemnatory, and the best they could offer was a scowl and the recommendation that the person exercise "self-control."

The incidence in Australia was not known. The Kinsey Report in the US estimated that 4 percent of males were exclusively homosexual, but that 37 per cent had some sort of homosexual experience between adolescence and old age. The Herald journalist added "the incidence in Australia may be a lot lower."

Letters, PEDAGOGUE. Recent scientific investigation of homosexual behaviour is most valuable and to be encouraged. But it is necessary to stress the lack of reliable statistics in this field. How is anybody to know how many homosexuals there are, and how many of the different kinds? The only ones who can be counted come to public clinics or fall into the hands of authorities.

We are told there are very few paedophiles, but who can know how many boys are solicited? Sometimes one might feel, after hearing of a series of solicitations, that there must be more than "a very few" paedophiles.

Moral failures in other fields are treated more leniently than for homosexuality. Therefore, some people argue, attitudes to homosexuality should be relaxed. But I disagree. Surely it is true that in this case, with these deviants, society must be prepared to protect its standards of sexual behaviour. To relax these standards must only encourage more of this deviant behaviour.

Letters, A Valley. People who are prepared to talk about the Wolfenden Report always end up talking about their experiences in public lavatories. But it is not only there that homosexual acts are done. I know of two doctors who meet regularly to do that, and also of two solicitors and a judge who meet for the same purpose. If I talk about this to anyone, they do not believe me because these men are regarded as being far above such depravity. But they are not. I wonder how much of it goes on in all the better parts of town as well among the workers.

Comment. When I read the Herald article and similar ones in other Papers, I thought that they would be flooded with Letters. Surely, given that the subject had been taboo for so long, bringing it to light now would rouse much comment from the community. But the Herald published only two Letters, shown above. The first dealt with the incidentals, like the statistics. The second raised another side to the matter.

But, I believe the issue simply was not yet ready to go on the public agenda. It was still all hush-hush, and really had to be lumped in with sex, religion and politics that no one talked about. It was not until 1978 that the first Sydney Mardi Gras parade was held, when, incidentally, 53 males were arrested. It was only later that "gays" started coming out of their closets. The first Australian jurisdictions to decriminalise homosexuality were the various Acts about 1975, and it took another ten or more years before **all** of the States followed suit. The point I am making here is that the social acceptance that is more-or-less evident now might have had its genesis in the events of the late fifties, but it took many years to come to maturity.

BYE BYE BILLY

Billy Graham going is home. Last night, five thousand people, including hundreds of weeping women, stood in heavy rain to farewell Dr Billy Graham, and to wish him a safe journey home.

Before he left, he addressed the crowd. He pointed out that during his visit, he had preached to 1,242,000 people, and 142,000 had Declared for God. Nevertheless, his campaign was 44,000 Pounds in the red. He went on to say that "we came here only as Christ's ambassadors. We shall certainly return and re-visit your wonderful country. But if I do not see you here again, I will see you up there", pointing heavenward.

After making his farewell to many individuals, many of them clergy, he waited at the plane door while the crowd sang *How Great Thou Art*, his tour theme song. And then, amid much sorrow in the crowd, he flew away.

Comment.   Most of the one-and-a-quarter million people who attended the Crusade would claim that it was a success. It certainly gave a short term boost to local Church attendances, though, from the few scattered statistics to be found, this boost scarcely carried over a year later. Opponents of Graham were little changed in their opinions. Dr E Burgmann, the widely-respected Anglican Bishop of Goulbourn, voiced his objections. He said that he could not go along with modern or fundamental campaigns, and the great Crusades did not provide the atmosphere for **serious** decisions. He also worried about how the Crusade would continue into the future. He thought that this type of Crusade, with all its flamboyance, would become institutionalised, quite separate from his existing Church, and would in fact further fragment the Christian faithful by giving them one more option.

He argued that Dr Graham's Crusade was a challenge to the existing Church, rather than to the world outside it. He added that the great majority of people who made a Decision for Christ were already practising Christians.

Of course, much of the evangelical and modernistic element has now been left behind by the Anglicans. It has not left Australia entirely, however, but has appeared with a lot of vigour in new forms of religious worship, in huge congregations in, for example, the Hillsong and other Churches round the nation.

WLADZIU VALENTINE LIBERACE

Liberace was born of Polish and Italian parents in Wisconsin in 1919. In his youth, he was often the subject of ridicule among his peers because of his overt and all-consuming devotion to music, his obsession with cooking and his rejection of all types of sport, including ..gasp.. baseball and American football. By the time he reached his majority, he was performing as a pianist in nightclubs and social functions, and was clearly headed for musical oblivion.

About 1940, he started to develop **a stage personality** that quickly brought him fame and fortune. **Firstly**, on the musical front, he forsook his oh-so-serious concentration on the classical masters, such as Chopin and Brahms, and instead created melodies that switched lightly from the classics to popular music, to hillbilly jaunts, and on to jazz and Chopsticks. At the same time he started to talk a ceaseless patter in a slow educated drawl that emphasised good American values and love for his mother, family and country.

Secondly he became, on stage, the consummate pansy. By his elaborate spangled clothing, his exaggerated female mannerisms, his soft caressing voice, his choice of music and his conversation rich in double entendres, he left no doubt as to his homosexuality.

This formula proved immensely popular. For forty years, from 1940 until his death in 1981, Liberace entertained, titillated and scandalised America and half the globe. This was a period when homosexuals were still "poofters" and had not been converted into "gays". Passions against them ran high across America, and Australia, and violence and prosecutions against them were common. Yet Liberace thrived in this atmosphere. His early attempts to star in the movies all failed, but his later TV shows were enormously successful, and his resident Los Vegas night-club act was a perpetual winner. To him, his alleged homosexuality might have had some downsides, but as he said "I cried all the way to the bank."

Was he a homosexual.? About 100 per cent of Americans would say he was. Also, in the long run, he died of complications from AIDS, a disease that is highly correlated in America with homosexuality. But against this is the fact that he always insisted that he was not. He also fought several court cases against allegations that he was, and won them all. And, for what it is worth, he was always keen on being seen in public with Hollywood's top starlets. So, perhaps he was, and perhaps he was not. And perhaps it does not matter.

Liberace in 1959. In 1956, Liberace had performed a series of concerts **in London**. His act had been reviewed by the fiery, irascible, super-critical critic William Connor, whose column appeared under the name Cassandra. Cassandra had not much liked what he saw. In fact, he tore the act and Liberace to shreds in as vitriolic a piece of writing as you will ever see published. The excerpt below speaks for itself.

Liberace is a deadly, winking, sniggering, snuggling, chromium-plated, scent-impregnated, luminous, quivering, giggling, fruit-flavoured, mincing, ice-covered heap of mother-love. He is the summit of sex, the pinnacle of masculine, feminine and neuter. Everything that he, she, and it, can want.
He reeks with emetic language that can only make grown men long for a quiet corner, an aspidistra, a handkerchief, and the old heave-ho. Without doubt, he is the biggest sentimental vomit of all time. Slobbering over his mother, winking at his brother, and counting the cash at every second, this superb piece of calculating candy-floss has an answer for every situation. There must be something wrong with us that our teenagers longing for sex, and our middle aged matrons fed up with sex alike, should fall for such a sugary mountain of jingling claptrap wrapped up in such a preposterous clown.

Liberace claimed that "fruit-flavoured' and "the summit of sex" references implied that he was a homosexual. He stated that he was against the practice of homosexuality because it offends convention, and it offends society.

Liberace sued Connor for libel. Connor (alias Cassandra), in the dock, played semantics on some leading questions. When asked what he meant by "the summit of sex" he replied that Liberace, by using his sex appeal, was the greatest exponent in show business, and had received audiences that were world records. He also said that "everything that he, or she, or it, can want" was a reference to the comprehensive nature of his technique – designed to apply to the whole of the community – the full circle. So, the first part of his legal position was that he had not consciously implied homosexuality at all.

Getting a bit closer to the point, he mainly based the rest of his defence on the argument that they were his honest opinions and that every Englishman had the right to express freely whatever he genuinely thought. People might think that he was wrong, but that was only their opinion. If you denied him the right of free expression because it gave offence to someone, then you removed one of the cornerstones of British justice and society.

Liberace was by the end of the trial's first week a major attraction for the London High Court. Women started queuing before seven in the morning, and the Court was full long before its hearings began. Liberace turned up respectfully attired, but with the flamboyance you might expect. For example on day five, he wore a copper-brown suit, made from a somewhat reflective material. He topped that off with gold cuff links and a gold wrist watch, all in the shape of a miniature grand piano.

As the case went on, a number of women came forward, and testified they had seen his show, and that they saw nothing offensive or dirty in it. He also enlisted the aid of a number of male theatre performers, and none of these latter persons gave any impression that they were in any way inclined to homosexuality.

In making his final submission, Mr Gilbert Beyfus, for Liberace, said it was time that Connor was taught to grasp the danger of words, and stop his incessant rudeness that apparently pays off so well in the journalistic profession. As for the Mirror newspaper, "it is violent and vicious, venomous and vindictive, salacious and sensational, ruthless and remorseless. Let your reward of damages be such a sum as will make the directors think when they deal with their balance sheets."

The judge came down strongly on the value of free speech. "We are all free to state such opinions in any way we like – diffidently, decorously, politely, or discreetly, or pungently, provocatively, rudely or even brutally. If the opinion is our real opinion honestly held and is such that any fair-minded man might honestly hold, then we are free to express them in any way we like." Given the conviction displayed by Cassandra, it now seemed likely that the jury would not find him guilty of **defamation**.

And that indeed was the result. Connor and the newspaper were found guilty on the charge of libel with respect to the implication of homosexuality, and not guilty on matters relating to libel in his attack on Liberace's performance. The culprits were fined 8,000 Pounds between them.

There were wild scenes as Liberace left the Court. Ushers and officials had to clear a way for him as people tried to clap him on the back, and shouted "well done." As the jostling, pushing crowd stopped traffic in the Strand, girls crowded round Liberace waving autograph books and scraps of paper.

"Liberace, in midnight-blue trousers and gold lame, was received with wild cheering and cries of "good on you, Libby" when he appeared at Chiswick Empire Theatre last night."

Comment. What good fun.

DANNY KAYE

Danny Kaye was in Australia to do a series of shows, that featured mainly himself talking "intimately" to his audience. In his time here, he was immensely popular with all who met him. He even charmed the Press. As for his shows, audiences were split. Either you liked him, or you hated him.

> **Letters, Laura Curtis.** Having been enchanted by Danny Kaye as a person and being an admirer of his talent and versatility, I am loath to express my extreme disappointment with the material used in his recent Sydney season. But who, oh who, was responsible for his script. Was it his usual bill-of-fare, or was it the old, old story of having been told that anything will do for us down under as we're a bunch of hicks and hayseeds.
>
> A little home-spun material can be delightful, but what a lot of it we got. The interminable audience-participation in singing and finger-snapping, the wads of blatant padding, the dollops of sheer corn, the unfunniness of the mercifully few topicalities. A charming and disarming personality doesn't quite make up for this.
>
> Just how brilliant he could have been was revealed in the superb mimicry of the satiric rendering of ballads sung in the English and German manner, and in the miming take-off of his supporting cast. But gems like these were wide apart in the low-carat setting.
>
> I should like to know if his script approximated one he would use to London or New York audiences. I rather suspect not. Poor old Aussies.
>
> **Letters, Margo Higgs.** With mounting indignation I read Laura Curtis's adverse criticism of Danny Kaye's performance. As a devoted admirer for many years,

and having seen all of his films, I was enraptured with each and every minute of his recent show. I can find no fault with Danny's superb showmanship and sheer warmth of personality.

A fellow-Englishman who had seen his performance at the Palladium in London tells me the Australian show was of exactly the same excellent calibre.

Letters, Heather Meers. Danny Kaye throws a similarly unworthy sop to his audiences in the United Kingdom too, and moreover, has been doing it for at least six years.

It was not until I had left the theatre that I remembered the words of an English friend describing Mr Kaye's lethargic performance some six years ago. As I read Laura Curtis's lament, I recognised the criticism as almost exactly that which she had made.

Perhaps my own judgement was slightly affected by the enormous distance at which I viewed the show, from the seat which management deigned to sell me for a trifling two Pounds, But I cannot help feeling that Mr Kaye was equally reprehensible.

NEWS AND VIEWS

Letters, S Johnston. Quite a lot has been written lately in the Press about the spread of disease through dirty hands. In one month, I have counted more than 50 people in business who lick or spit on their finger before picking up a piece of paper. These include butchers, bakers, people handling small-goods, etc.

One woman wrapping sandwiches licked her fingers every time she reached for a piece of tissue paper. Other finger-lickers include bank clerks, girls in offices giving change, railway ticker sellers, bookmakers issuing tickets, and their clerk paying out money.

Letters, Philip Bird. Mr M Bruxner, in the legislative Assembly, of the dangers of crossing dingoes with Alsatians, said that the dingo originated with the wolf.

I think that if Mr Bruxner inquires a little further he will find nothing is known of when or from where the dingo came. It is believed by most competent authorities that the dingo came to Australia with the Aborigines.

Letters, P Kemp, Armidale. The other day I rang a certain hotel in Grafton to arrange accommodation. After a tedious five-minute wait the telephonist returned to the line to inform me that the line did not seem to be answering. "Well" I said, "that's impossible, the number is a hotel." Immediately the telephonist broke in assuredly: "Oh, well, if that's the case, they'll all be away at the races today."

Do you think that this is typical of the service in Australian hotels?

Letters, OLD BUSHMAN. Until about 12 years ago, I always wore shoes made of kangaroo hide. I could always buy them in Hurstville until I went to buy a pair one day and the gentleman said there would be no more kangaroo hide shoes because America had cornered all the hides. It seems he was right, as some American papers advertise the shoes and handbags and other goods made from Australian kangaroos, which they describe as the best leather in the world for making these kinds of articles.

There would be plenty of shooters if the Government would give a fair price for the hides. Any good shooter would make more than 100 Pounds per week.

I would suggest sending a few soldiers out of the Army. It would be good rifle practice, and would do a good turn for the farmers.

JULY: MAX STUART'S TRIALS

On Saturday, December 20, 1958, Rupert Maxwell Stuart was a 27-year-old aborigine working on a darts stall at the Funland Carnival at Ceduna, 480 miles from Adelaide. At about four o'clock, he left the fair, and started the search for alcoholic drinks.

Sadly, though, a small white girl, aged 9 years, was raped and murdered in a cave a mile away, between 2pm and 4pm. Stuart was apprehended by police, and initially gave the above account of his movements, but subsequently he dictated and signed a confession of guilt. He was charged with the crime, and at the subsequent trial in April, was found guilty.

He was granted leave to appeal, and after the appeal failed, he was sentenced to hang on May 22. In the meantime, agitation was growing in the community over the police and the Court procedures that had been followed, and many were prepared to claim that justice had been denied to Stuart.

The main claim was the Stuart had been found guilty only because of his alleged confession. For example, he had written;

Court records. She was standing in a pool of water, playing. I said to the little girl "there is some little birds over there". I pointed up towards the cave. She said "I will go there and have a look." She walked into the cave. No, I am wrong. I crawled in the cave first and she crawled after me. She said "where's the birds?" and I said "they are gone now" I punched her on the side of the head. She went unconscious. I took her bathers off. Then I raped her. She was hard to root. I done her. Then I hit her on the head with a stone.

The growing number of defenders of Stuart's rights were convinced that Stuart, who was scarcely literate, did not have the language capacity to dictate such a clear and coherent account. They claimed that the police had either written it themselves, or dictated it to him for writing. But, on the other hand, the police were adamant that Stuart had dictated it voluntarily and that it was **entirely** his work. It was this insistence on their behalf, in the face of Stuart's obvious near-illiteracy, that badly weakened the case they brought against him. He appealed to the High Court, but to no avail, except that it delayed the execution for a few weeks.

By the time we take up the story in early July, some authorities were having second thoughts.

> **Press reports, Saturday, July 7**. A number of people are telephoning the South Australian Government in a bid to save the life of a man due to be hanged next Tuesday. They have offered some 200 Pounds towards an appeal to the Privy Council for Max Stuart, a seven-eights aboriginal. Such an appeal would cost an estimated 2,000 Pounds, and it appears likely that the State would share no part of this cost.
>
> The calls follow action by the Federal Opposition Leader, Dr Evatt, who sent a telegram to Premier Playford asking that the death sentence be commuted to life imprisonment. In this telegram, he referred to the fact that certain features of the case caused the High Court some anxiety.
>
> He went on to say that "their unusual comments are of great significance. The High Court judgment showed that Stuart was convicted entirely because of a confession typed by police officials and signed by the accused in block letters. It has been sworn before the

High Court that the confession could not have been dictated by a totally illiterate aborigine."

A few days later, there was an unusual plea for finance.

Letters, July 11. Rev Frank Coaldrake, Chairman Australian Board of Missions. The Law Society of South Australia has already received over 500 Pounds of the 2,000 Pounds needed for an appeal to the Privy Council for Max Stuart, convicted of murder. Stuart is sentenced to death, but a further two weeks reprieve has been granted to consider making the appeal. The appeal will be made if the money can be raised. Some of your readers will surely feel moved to send a cheque to the Law Society, 26 Pirie Street, Adelaide.

The youthful Rupert Murdoch was then owner of the Age, his sole newspaper in Adelaide. He had joined the ranks of supporters of Stuart, and was advocating strongly for his reprieve through his own columns. He and his editor, the now famous Rohan Rivett, arranged to send a Catholic priest, Father Tom Dixon, to the Atherton Tablelands in Queensland, to find the Funland Carnival. They hoped he would be able to find witnesses that corroborated Stuart's story. He was able to do that, when he found two women and a man who had held adjacent stalls to Stuart back in Ceduna, and these averred that Stuart had been at his stall from 2pm to 4pm on the day of the murder.

These three people each signed statutory declarations that went along these lines.

Edna Gieseman, Declaration. I, Edna Gieseman, do solemnly and sincerely declare that Rupert Max Stuart is well known to me. On Saturday, December 20, Max came back to our caravan about 1.45pm. We had just finished dinner and the girls had just finished washing up and wiping the table.

I told him he should be on time for his meals and he said he was sorry. He handed me five shillings to get some beer and wine for him, I refused, and told him to get Betty Gadd to get it for him. I told Betty Hopes to give him some bread and butter and vegetables, which he had.

Betty Gadd arrived back in a taxi with a bottle of beer and a bottle of wine. I could not let him drink the beer and the wine, but put them in the caravan and told him to work the stall, which he did.

He took about four Pounds between then and when he left the park between 4pm and 4.30pm. Allen Moir went with him.

I did not see Max Stuart again till next morning, when he was sober and cleaned up, and he told me he had a job in Ceduna and was staying on.

On Saturday night, I had searched for both Max and Alan, as we wanted to pull down the show. But could not find them around town, and I went along to the pictures and put an advert on the screen, but this did not bring them.

The other two statutory declarations told a similar story. They were telegraphed through to Playford, and he agreed to hold over the execution for another four weeks. They were also telegraphed to the Privy Council where the appeal was under way. Here, however, the judges remained unmoved by this new evidence, as their role was to evaluate the original trial for irregularities, and they were not free to delve into any old or new evidence presented. After a brief consultation, for which they did not leave the Courtroom, the Five Lords denied Stuart the right to again appeal against his sentence.

But by now, there was too much heat for Playford to ignore. Within a few days, he announced a Royal Commission into the whole matter. There were many people (including Murdoch) who said the three Commissioners were hand-picked simply to confirm the death penalty on Stuart. There were also many (including Murdoch) who said that Playford was playing to his political image of hard-liner, tough on crime. After all, his Government had already executed seven persons. Whatever the truth of these allegations, Max Stuart was granted a stay of execution for a few months longer.

We will pick up his harrowing story at that time.

THE COLD WAR IS WARM AGAIN

Relations between America and Russia were no better and no worse than they had been for a decade and more. Each of them still wanted to be seen as the good guy who was, nevertheless, incredibly tough and invincible when provoked. They both were happy to give large sums of monies to smaller countries to persuade them to join their own bloc, and even happier to subvert any government or agency that got in their way. At the diplomatic level, they walked out of conferences, disrupted meetings with silly claims, and above all, threatened all and sundry with atomic and many other charming forms of oblivion.

For example, in only a few days early in July, the Russians were clearly in a belligerent mood.

Khrushchev, the Soviet Prime Minister: If the Soviet Union and the United States did come into conflict, the result would be a terrible calamity, because if we fight there is no force on earth that could stop Russia

Khrushchev again: the Communist camp has grown so powerful that it has all the means necessary to halt the American warmongers. We say this to German Chancellor Adenauer, ... if you or America try to raise your hand against the countries of the Socialist camp, we will break you. The lovers of military adventures must be very careful; they have to reckon with the forces of Communism which are stronger now than ever before.

More classic Khrushchev: Your generals talk of maintaining your position in Berlin by force. This is a bluff. If you send in tanks, they will burn. Make no mistake about it. If you want war, you can have it, but remember it will be your war. Our rockets will fly automatically.

The Americans responded with their own forms of eloquence, and in turn were as obstructive as they could be without provoking a real crisis. For example, in the previous October, the Russians had ceased nuclear testing, and proposed that Americans do likewise. The US eventually fell in with this, but when the Russians proposed a permanent ban on nuclear testing, they dragged their feet, and delayed making a decision long enough to make the Russian proposal lapse. In the meantime, they had spent all the months when the ban was in operation preparing vast catacombs in the Nevada desert ready for the next round of testing. Not that this was all **that** bad; given that the Russians were making the same preparations back home.

It seemed that, in matters of policy, there was no consistency. It was government by the seat of the pants. Let me emphasise this by two examples. **For example,** in the same speech that Khrushchev threatened to annihilate America, he mellowed and talked about how good it would be if Eisenhower would visit Russia. "It would not be a bad idea if your President came here, and I visited the United States. If the Soviet and US remained friends, there could never be a war. If someone else starts a war, then together we could stop it. We highly valued your friendship during the War, when we fought a common enemy – Germany. I said I had the highest respect for Eisenhower then and I have now. During the war, he acted like a real gentleman. We had no frictions then, but now relations are bad, and we'd like to return to old times."

Comment. This was the Cold War. It had been going on for over a decade, and would go on for a few more decades. Right now, it was in a nice, benign period. At other times, it heated up, and threats of nuclear destruction flew backwards and forwards with gay abandon. Once, in the Cuban Missile Crisis in 1961, the two belligerent nations actually might have had a nuclear incident. But generally, they were content to strut and bluff and make a lot of noise, knowing or hoping that the other guy, the bad guy, had enough sense to avoid a conflict that would have destroyed everyone.

At the time, I was in my mid-twenties. To me, the Cold War appeared a joke. I too thought that no one would press the trigger because the consequences would have been so horrible. Even during the Cuban Crisis, I wrongly thought it was all just more propaganda. Of course at that age, I was clearly indestructible, and had nothing to fear from anything. I know that there were people round who took the War seriously, but since I was never going to die, why should I worry about all that stuff? Younger people than me were more impressed by it, and now many of them feel that they grew up in the shadow of a nuclear holocaust, and recall with amazing accuracy some of the events of those days.

So, my advice to you is that once you get to 25 years of age, you should stay right there, and then never have to worry about anything again.

MORE INNOVATIONS ON THE WAY

Complete digital dialing. Prior to this, Sydney's phone numbers had two letters followed by four digits. For example, XB6472. But now, the first two letters were to be replaced by two digits, so that the number became six digits. The system was soon to be extended to the country areas. So that Kurri Kurri 128, on a manual exchange, was soon also to be automated to an all-digital number.

Not everyone thought this was progress.

Letters, B Schumacher. The PMG's increasing use of all-digit telephone numbers and figures does not seem to be popular with any of the most important people, that is, the telephone users. Apart from the "other cities use this system, so it must be good" type of argument, no reason has been advanced good enough to justify this retrograde step.

Letters, B Bailey. How can anyone remember six numbers. I can hardly manage four, but I manage. I can always remember the first two letters because I tie them up with people's names. The next thing we know, the exchanges will get overloaded and we will have seven numbers and then even eight. The human brain can only remember so much.

Let me point out that someone had pointed out to me that there are a possible 676 "combinations" of two letters, and only a hundred "combinations" of two numbers. Why not do the obvious thing and make the phone numbers all letters, and no numbers. That would reduce the size of the phone number to about half.

Comment. With the introduction of changes to the phone system, thousands of women gradually lost their jobs at local exchanges, and one source of wonderful stories about the old phone system dried up.

Self-service petrol. Press Report. An application to install self-serve petrol pumps in NSW threatens a major political storm. A Melbourne Company, Engineering Products P/L has made the application to the NSW Minister for Labour and Industry. The government will be under intense industrial pressure to refuse the application.

Self-service pumps would enable motorists to obtain petrol 24 hours of the day, even on Sundays. A motorist would be able to put any number of two shilling pieces, up to one Pound, in a slot on the wall of the service station. He would then feed petrol from a standard pump to their petrol tanks. The supply would cut off automatically when the amount of petrol paid for had been fed to the petrol tank.

The pumps are opposed by the Unions because they fear that they would put many people out of work. They would also cut across the government's plan to licence service stations, a plan being put forward to prevent them from trading after hours.

An MLA with close Union ties said that if they do not stop these moves somewhere, no one can tell where the operation of vending machines will end. It could come to the stage where groceries could be sold through them at any hour.

Press report. The NSW Government has asked the Mines Department to investigate the proposed self-service pumps to see whether they constitute a fire hazard. There are fears that a spillage might by ignited by a cigarette, and an explosion of fire might result.

At the same time, the State Liberal Party decided unanimously to support their introduction. Also the Fire and Accident Underwriters association of Australia had approved their use throughout Australia. They point out that ninety of them are operating in Victoria and Tasmania, and no incident of fire, accident or vandalism concerning them has been reported.

Press Reports. Parking Meters in Manly. After a heated two-hour debate last night, Manly Council decided by seven votes to four to install parking meters in the Manly business area. About 200 meters will now be installed as soon as the decision is ratified.

A record crowd of 52, mainly business people, packed the public gallery, and heckled speakers who supported the motion.

Alderman D Williams, who was **for** the motion, said "it is an unpopular action. Areas which have meters are better controlled. It is an initial shock, but Manly must be prosperous. I feel we must give the idea a trial."

On the other hand, Alderman D Whittle said "Parking meters have proved disastrous to business in other areas. I do not know what the answer is, but I am convinced that meters are not in Manly's best interests."

The Mayor, W Fairbairn, said that in Brisbane the idea had been so successful that they were installing another 150 meters.

The Tote is coming, Press report, July 28. The only form of betting on horse racing in any State was at the race track. There, people could gamble legally with a bookie, or with an on-course machine called a totalisator. However, outside the racetracks were vast networks of bookies and punters who every race day bet enormous sums of money **illegally**. This so-called SP system of betting **spanned the nation**, there were bookies in every pub and club in every small town in the nation. These punters were constantly harassed by local police and by Flying Squads, and the bookies were regularly booked and charged with illegal gambling.

At this time, pressure was growing to replace this illegal system with a legal one. The great motivator for change for the State Governments was that they would then hope that illegal gambling would die out, and that they – the Governments – would gain much taxation by getting a cut of the revenue that changed hands.

So the day was fast approaching when totalisators (soon to become TABs) would be introduced. Various Enquiries had been held in the different States, and Victoria appeared to be about the first to give it a go. Strong forces were lined up against it, including the Churches who mostly said that it would encourage gambling, and thus they opposed it. Many others approved of the new scheme, including the bulk of the punters, who simply preferred an open legal scheme, operating in respectable premises, to one that was conducted in the lavatories of pubs and parked cars outside them.

In any case, within a year the major States were well under way with implementing the system. Needless to say, since then, the States have indeed cashed in on the revenue, and the TABs have extended their domain to include gambling on all sorts of football, cricket, and of course, those two flies crawling up the wall.

The new Boeing 707. Here is another wonderful bit of new technology. The trouble was that it came with a pollution problem. Of course, back in 1959, the environment was not such an issue. The noise generated by the plane **was** seen as a problem. It was also true that traffic had to be stopped on certain roads for some minutes while it took off, so that the ascending plane would not come too close.

But **the smoke**, while objected to by some, **was not a big concern.**

ILLEGITIMATE CHILDREN

A bastard child, to put it simply, in 1959 was a child conceived out of wedlock. Probably the most common form of this was with a young girl entering a sexual relationship, and then suffering the "shame" of giving birth to an illegitimate child. Often the whole event was somehow hushed up, and there were plenty of "Aunties" in the country and the city who can attest to this as the girl came for a prolonged visit. But in any case, the child was born with a stigma, a social stigma. Throughout life, particularly childhood, it bore the epithet of "bastard" and its social standing was well below par.

With the coming of the 1960's, things started to change. Along with the re-growth of aggressive feminism and of the drug culture, there was the beginning of the gradual and slow emergence of new cohorts of young people, some of whom rejected the institution of marriage, and who chose to bear and raise children outside of wedlock. In any case, the classification of children as bastards, and as being illegitimate, was removed from the Statute books in Australia in the 1970's, in all States except Western Australia.

Comment. The above examples should show you, as if you needed showing, just how much times have changed.

THE GREATEST VEHICLE OF ALL TIMES

By 1959, tens of thousands of young adults were making new nests for themselves and buying up big on houses, Hills Hoists, lawn mowers, and anything that the great system of HP would allow. Mortgages had reached levels that made the bankers happy, and discussion of second mortgages kept Saturday-night dinner parties lively.

There was one item lacking from the above list, and that was the motor car. Every family had to get one, and once garaged, it virtues had to be defended against all comers.

There were certain types of cars that were socially acceptable. Australian-made cars were OK, British cars were more prestigious, but it was well know they did not perform so well. European vehicles were high quality, but they were expensive, and besides European people were a bit suspect, so only the older, more remote, people bought them. Mind you, VW's were OK. There were no Jap cars.

American yank-tanks were powerful but most of them had good names and nothing else. They were petrol guzzlers, and their wings were pretentious. Only for mug lairs.

On balance, the Holden Family wagon was about the best. It held three kids easily, with the room for more animals in the back. Both the two-legged and four-legged variety. It was reasonably priced, and of course, it was Australian made.

What more could you ask?

LICENCED TO KILL

It was 1959. I was 25 years of age. At about this time I wanted a **motor bike** licence. After I had held my Permit for while, I drove to Kurri Kurri Police Station, and the Sergeant was out the front, and saw me arrive. He must have thought I could ride well enough, because he invited me inside. He asked if I had read the Rule Book, and when I said "yes", he took my money and said I would get the paper work in a few weeks. I did not look at it for a month, and when I did, it was a licence to **drive a car**. I took it back to the sergeant, and told him. He asked me to give it to him. He pulled out his fountain pen, and scratched out "DRIVER" and wrote "RIDER" in its stead. And that was that.

Times **have** changed.

GETTING A HOUSE: A PERSONAL MEMORY

In 1959, I had been married about five years ago, and had a beautiful wife and two children that were partly civilised. I was changing jobs and the meant I had to vacate a house I was living in, and so I decided that it was now time to join the throng and buy a house.

Like so many other innocents at the time, I thought a good way to go was to buy a block of land, and get a project home built on it. There were many project builders around, and quite a few of them seemed honest enough to tempt me.

So, my wife and I did our sums, put on our best clothes, and went to see our bank manager at the Commonwealth. We had banked there all our lives, and were confident that would help us get a loan. And indeed we would, we were told. All we had to do was keep saving at our current rate for another five years, and we could then get a loan of 70 per cent of our estimated price.

So, we were in a trap. If we followed this path, we would have to go to rented digs, and that would stop us from saving at the required rate.

After messing round with other financial institutions, we tried the Rural bank. This was a body that was owned at the time by the NSW Government, and which we thought would be as stuffy as the Commonwealth. We were greeted there by a Mr Smith, and that in itself was suspicious.

He listened sympathetically to our plight, pretending that he had not heard it all hundreds of times, and then said that we could have the loan. Not only that, he offered us another 700 Pounds to furnish it and buy a Hills Hoist.

What a Champion. Granted the loan was a rate one percentage point higher then the Commonwealth, and the extra 700 Pounds was at Hire Purchase rates. He was still a champion.

So with this backing behind us, we approached a few project builders. We settled on one that offered a house-and-land package **off a standard design with no changes**. It was on a cliff in a small jungle, but it turned out to be a nice comfortable house that only went about six months overtime in the building.

Just after we our took possession of the new house, the builder went into liquidation, and so dozens of others, just behind us in the queue, lost their deposits at least. This, it was just being realised, was one of the hazards of these small project builders, and so the giants like Lend Lease quickly dominated the scene.

There were tens of thousands of other young couple just like us who were taking the same risks as we were at the time. Being young and quite foolish, it all seemed like a big adventure, and we were quite lucky to come out of it unscathed. At the time, horror stories took up hours of Saturday dinner-table talk, and if you did not have a rattling good mortgage story to tell, you were left out.

It should be remembered that while all this home-building was going on for some people, there were over half a million people who were quite immune from any such frivolity. These were people who had been renting a dwelling in 1940, and **who had seen no rent increases since that date. Commonwealth and States laws protected them from this nuisance.** What a racket.

And this lasted in the major States until about 1966.

AUGUST: ROYAL COMMISSION

By the end of July, Max Stuart knew a lot more about Australia's legal system than he knew at the beginning of the month. He was still incarcerated, he was still accused of murder, and he was by no means on good terms with the Premier or the authorities. Yet, over the month, a few things had gone his way.

Firstly, on July 31, Premier Playford announced that he was appointing a Royal Commission to look into aspects of the case. And that meant that Stuart's execution was postponed for another month.

Secondly, the State Opposition had now become involved, and in its own inevitable way, it had done so by saying that whatever the Government did, it was wrong. This meant that, while they did not say at all that Stuart was innocent, they would become very active in criticising the Government for the processes involved in the Commission. Given that the President of the Opposition Labor Party was Don Dunstan, a lawyer, and later himself to become a Premier of the State, it was unlikely that any untoward matters would escape critical scrutiny. On top of that, remember that newspaper publisher Rupert Murdoch was also watching, protecting the rights of Stuart. It would have been hard to find two more competent watchdogs than this pair.

The Opposition were concerned early with two issues. They contended that the police had made reckless statements about the condemned man's legal status and background that were quite inconsistent with the evidence. The second point they initially raised was the curious truth that the

South Australian Department of Aborigines had been strangely absent from the case, whereas it might have been expected that they would have been prominent in offering their services. Neither of these allegations resounded well in the general community.

Another hard thing for the populace to swallow was that the Chairman of the Commission, Sir Maurice Napier, was also the Chief Justice of South Australia. It was hard to argue that such a person was always at arms length from Government. Also, that the second judge was Mr Justice Reid, who had been the judge at Stuart's original trial. Again, it was easy to doubt impartiality. Another, perhaps specious, objection was that none of the three judges had any experience in Aboriginal affairs.

There were so many grey areas where the Commission was open to attack. Just as one example, see this brief interchange over the lack of aboriginal experience of the Commissioners. In the long run, this was small beer, but a multitude of such arguments weakened the credibility of the inquiry.

> **Letter to *SMH*, A Nulty, Aug 27.** Your editorial of a day ago questioned the impartiality of the Commission. And there is also the extraordinary statement that "none of the Commission has had any experience of dealing with partly civilised aborigines."
>
> The Commissioners, all trained men of high legal standing, have to weigh evidence for and against the accused; the question of race or colour does not come into the matter. What help could an anthropologist or missionary give to them?
>
> **The Editor replied.** Our leading article specifically questioned, not the impartiality of the Commissioners,

but the essential **appearance** of incontestable impartiality, which **many people believe is lacking in the whole procedure**. What is alarming is not that the doubts are justified, but that they exist. As to experience of Aborigines, this is not a question of race or colour, but of language and psychological approach.

As it turned out, as the Commission progressed, these judges behaved quite properly, and there was no legitimate reason to complain. Still, at the very beginning it was easy to stir up passions by raising doubts as to their probity.

A third point for Stuart was that the Premier announced that his Government was prepared to pay the expenses of all those called before the enquiry. Since many of the witnesses that favoured Stuart were now somewhere in the region of North Queensland, with their travelling fair, this was good news.

The final piece of glad tidings was that Jack Shand, a famous barrister from Sydney, agreed to appear for Stuart. Shand had built an enormous reputation for himself, in an earlier Royal Commission, by arguing successfully that his client Frederick McDermott was innocent of the murder for which he had been gaoled five years previously. So, there was no doubt that Stuart then had the very best defence.

The Commission got seriously underway in mid-August. The early days were quiet and predictable. Witnesses were called, some of whom said they had seen Stuart at various times at the fair, and others who said they had not. All of these were too vague, as regards time, to sway matters one way or another. One witness caused a bit of a stir by telling of how he was given ten Shillings by a detective after he signed a statement that Stuart had confessed privately to him. This allegation did gain some attention, but was not given much credence as true evidence.

But, in mid-August, when Shand was to introduce three, more weighty, witnesses, he was given permission to introduce only one. The next morning, he re-appeared in Court, and after four minutes, walked out and went back to Sydney. He was of the opinion that "we are not being given, nor will be given, a thorough investigation into this matter. We consider that our continued association with the Commission will in no way help Stuart, and will in fact, hinder him. This Commission is unable to consider properly the problems before it and we therefore withdraw."

This bombshell threw the Commission into confusion. Stuart added to that by saying he did not want another, different Counsel. No government wanted to proceed with an illiterate aborigine representing himself as a defendant in a murder trial. What a scandal that would raise. So at the end of the month, they were hard at work to bring Stuart back into the legal fold.

Shand himself got some tough criticism for walking out. For example, J Brazel, the Assistant Commissioner, said that "the move was made on the flimsiest of justifications, for his misconduct". He added that Shand was "guilty of a grave dereliction of duty." The Bar Council in each of the States met, and after much ado, each decided that it did not have enough information to either condemn or condone the action, and issued statements to that affect. But, it soon became of reduced importance to Shand, because he regrettably died of cancer on October 20th.

One consequence of these manoeuvres was that Stuart was granted another reprieve for a month, until past the end of September. In the meantime, he was living full time with the shadow of death creeping just in front of him, always hoping that it would somehow go away. But for the time being, that would have to satisfy him. The whole process was substantially delayed by Shand's departure, and we will take the story up again in October.

MEN IN OFFICES UNDER THE HAMMER

Men working in big offices in 1959 were on sacred ground, and **there was much prestige to working there**. Young people often simply aspired to "work in an office", and that was seen as being a satisfactory career path.

But not every one admired all aspects of the much-hallowed workers, as shown by the two ladies below. The first of these is a bit garbled in places, but she bares her fangs remarkably well, and we are not left in doubt as to what she meant.

Letters, (Miss) Nerol Whittle. Like the Kyoto machine you mentioned in your Editorial, Poor Obsolete Miss Brown can also transcribe the Japanese writing of her boss into Roman letters, and his four-plums-in-his-mouth voice into English words. Further, Miss Brown, who "goes into daily retirement behind her spectacles, and who laughs in her sleep", always knows where the largest vacuum in the office is located.

If Australian men, who know perfectly well that there is no room for improvement, had to speak their letters into a machine, clear speech would become a necessity, and speech training an imperative subject in a business course for city men and executives. Most men would have to leave the office suddenly to imbibe some Dutch courage to help them face "that infernal machine" for they would be as terrified of it as they were of their first schoolmistresses, and as they would be of their capable typists.

Businessmen are not university dons. They do not think quickly or express themselves concisely. They state, hesitate, re-state, mumble and jumble, and are often at a loss that they must perforce look to Miss Brown to supply the better word, the more apt expression, the happier turn of phrase. (After all, dammit, that's what she's paid for!) The Master Mind, having delivered himself of a few poorly constructed replies to the morning's correspondence, passes the whole sheet over to Miss Brown to compose.

Had the superiority of women as workers not been so obvious, the office work of the world would be done by typists with beards and moustaches. Poor Miss Brown is indispensable. Poor, helpless, forgettable, unmethodical and merely silly man can not get through his exhausting (?) day at the office without her.

Letters, Adrienne Smith. As your basic English conversation has shown itself of accepting the shock of brilliant colours and new materials in men's suits over the past few years, mightn't it also be able to stand the shock of discarding the suit itself?

In a climate far removed from the drizzling monotony of cool England, our menfolk swelter for most of the year, while we women-folk are free to weary breezy short, sleeveless dresses and sandals. Imagine the outcry there would be from us if we were forced by convention to wear long sleeves, tight collars, ties, and heavy shoes in the heat of summer.

Even the introduction of light-weight wools for mens' suits does not alter the fact that the suit itself is not designed for this country.

Comment. I leave it to readers to argue for themselves whether the situation has improved for men in big offices. But I am reminded that the Don Dunstan, mentioned above in connection with Max Stuart, later became Premier of South Australia. It turned out he was a popular and successful leader. But his moments of greatest fame arrived when he publicly supported male dress reform, and began appearing in public in a safari suit, with hot pink shorts, very short and very tight. Needless to say, this was a fad that did not survive.

A LOT OF TALK ABOUT WAR

I mentioned above that the Cold War was everywhere. To make the point of how pervasive it was, I include a few quite different examples of how it kept popping up all over the place.

Press Release, US Department of Civil Defence, New York. A young couple and their three children yesterday emerged from 14 day's isolation in a bathroom sized atomic shelter without electricity and running water. They had volunteered as human guinea pigs for the Department of Civil Defence. The purpose of the experiment was to determine whether people could survive the experience of an atomic attack, and in what condition they would emerge. They were well paid for doing the trial, and their payment increased with every day they spent in the shelter, up to 14 days.

A double bed was provided for the children and individual mattresses for the parents. Candles and torches provided evening lighting. A chemical toilet and jars of water and canned and packaged food provided the luxuries. There was no radio or TV, though they did have a voluminous library. A panic button was on standby if they wanted an early release.

They came out of the shelter in good condition, and were declared to be in good health by medical authorities. The test was welcomed as a complete success.

Press report, Washington, Sept 1. The human race could survive atomic war despite the genetic effects of radiation, says a report by the Joint Congressional Committee on Atomic Energy.

The Committee investigated the hypothetical case of 263 nuclear bombs delivered on 224 specified targets in the US. It was calculated that under present conditions, such an attack would have the cost of 50 million lives with about 20 million others sustaining serious injuries.

More than one-fourth of the dwellings in The States would have been destroyed, and 10 million others damaged. Another 13 million homes would have been severely contaminated by radio-active fall-out.

This maximum cost could be reduced by providing high-performance shelter protection for 200 million people at about 1000 million dollars.

W C (Billy) Wentworth, St Andrew's Cathedral, Luncheon Club. This noted firebrand argued that Australia could survive only under one of two scenarios. **The first** would be if a world-wide system of international control of all nations was established This would involve Australia surrendering her sovereignty to a higher international body, and obeying the instructions handed down. **Comment.** Not really likely

The second was that Australia, and other countries, go it alone and get the bomb for her own protection. "There are currently only three countries, Britain, Russia and America, in the nuclear Club, but that number is certain to rise quickly. It may be only 20 years before most countries have entered the Club."

Comment. Since then, the Club has picked up quite a few members. But not Australia. Given that there are already over 100,000 nuclear bombs in the world today, it seems we might not worry too much about joining. Perhaps we could just borrow them.

ABC Guest of Honour. Rear Admiral Bertram Taylor said last night that **sea battles of the future** might be fought entirely under water, by nuclear submarines. With new equipment, hull forms, weapons and methods of detecting targets, the submarine of today has a far greater potential than its predecessors in WWII. To all of this has been added nuclear propulsion with its almost unlimited endurance. "In the future we will see submarines armed with guided missiles with nuclear warheads....I don't think that all future ships in navies will be submarines, but I'm certain that submarines will form a high proportion, and possess powers far greater than their numbers suggest."

Comment. Rear-Admiral Taylor brought home to this nation the rapidly growing importance of nuclear submarines in war. Nuclear submarines were still in their infancy, and were generally thought of as being nuclear only in the sense of their **propulsion.** It was a big step, now introduced by Taylor, to see them as nuclear in **the sense of weapons**.

RSL National President, Sir George Holland, claimed that not one in 10,000 Australians had the slightest inkling of **how to protect himself in the event of a nuclear attack**. He went on to say that there was a lack of unity and liaison in the nation's civil defence system. He wanted youths, not required for national service training under the present system, to be called up for civil defence training to form the nucleus of a nation-wide civil defence organisation.

Comment. These are just a few examples of how the Cold War propaganda was flowing day in and day out. I did a survey of the first four pages of three major metropolitan newspapers over ten days, and just on half of the column-inches were taken up **with war talk in one form or another**. But, as I mentioned above, it was like water off a duck's back for most people. "Ho Hum" they said, and talked about the week-end footie, and Princess Alexandra's tough schedule.

FLIMSY STOCKINGS

Letters, D Cornmell, Treasurer, Our Girls Watching Society, City North Division, Mosman. One of the few simple joys permitted the family man in this drab age is – or should I say, was – to see the silky shine of a shapely feminine calf sheathed in vintage 15-or-better denier nylon. But the fact is that stairways, footpaths and even open Continental car doors are just NOT revealing beauty as a joy for ever to our oldest and steadiest members.

The view is aesthetically ruined by repellent ladders, runs, snags, pull holes, and signs of wholesale disintegration. Worse, the dowager from Pymble appears to accept this state of affairs, along with the duchess from Panania, as being part of life, like the weather forecasts.

Sir, our members do now make formal protest at this stab in the back from stocking manufacturers. Further we respectively recommend to the thousands of those delightful owners of those (hitherto) shapely calves, that they go stockingless for one week per fortnight until our exploiters restore quality.

Letters, SICK OF LADDERS. I agree with your writer about the very poor lasting quality of nylons.

Where are the good-quality nylons that we knew some years ago? Why has the lasting quality deteriorated and why is it that those from the USA (eagerly sought after by visitors to the country) far outlast anything manufactured here?

Some time ago I was asked to help collect old nylons for a charity, and was staggered at the heaps and heaps we collected which were obviously worn once or twice (as the feet were perfectly good). But the ladders and snags told their own story, that the owners must have had to dispose of them long before they should have done.

I work in a large office, and it is nothing to hear the girls complain that they have to buy stockings twice a week.

It would be interesting to hear from hosiery manufacturers themselves as to why nylons have not the lasting properties of (say) the Perlons made in West Germany, which give three of four times the wear (even the finest denier) of nylons made here.

This is not a new subject. I can recall your paper some years back printed quite a number of letters of complaint on the same subject, so it is something the manufacturers have had plenty of time to remedy.

ALBERT NAMATJIRA

News report. This evening, Aboriginal artist, Albert Namatjira suffered a heart attack at the Papunya Native Welfare Centre. He was carried by ambulance 170 miles to hospital in Alice Springs. On arrival, he rallied for a short time, but died later at 8pm. He was surrounded by his family and friends, and his death was peaceful.

News of his death spread in one hour throughout the length and breadth of the Northern Territory, and there was genuine and heartfelt sorrow everywhere. Tears were shed by many people who had never even met him.

Many prominent Australians reacted with sorrow to his death, including Frank Clune. He said "Poor Albert, he was the most outstanding aboriginal this country has produced. He had the bone pointed at him, and he died of a broken heart. Albert should be buried alongside John Flynn in the shadow of Mount Gillen."

William Dobell was "very sorry to hear of Albert's passing. I admired him as a man, and as an artist. I feel that the unfortunate treatment he has received recently may have hastened his death."

Namatjira's death occurred just two months after he was released from detention at Papunya Reserve. He had served three months detention there for having supplied a native with liquor.

SEPTEMBER: KINGSGROVE SLASHER

Kingsgrove, in 1959, was a very nice, middle-class, sleepy suburb, twelve miles from the centre of Sydney. One of its inhabitants was a David Joseph Scanlon. He had been born in Taree, and had lived in Sydney since he was nine. He attended school at Paddington and Kogarah, and had worked for 13 years with an importing and general warehouse company, earning 16 Pounds per week. He was married, and lived in pretty suburbs like Lavender Bay. He he was highly regarded by his employer, and well liked by everyone who knew him.

Here, apparently, was a good quite citizen in steady work, and living the quiet, contented life of the suburbs. But, it turned out, from 1956 to 1958, he developed a habit that distinguished him from all other men in that he slipped out at night, and roamed far and wide through neighbouring suburbs, and silently entered many houses. When inside, he went into the bedroom of a lady or a female child, and after a while they awoke, to their horror, to find that he had violated them in some way. Often, he slashed their bedclothes with a long razor or short knife. One 15-year-old girl told the Court that she had woken to find an arm across her neck and chest. She could not see anything. She screamed and heard her mother scream. The blanket and top sheet of her bed had been cut, and there were bruises and fingernail marks on her chest. The physical damage he did was generally slight, but the shock he induced in victims was extreme.

Needless to say, he then made a quick exit, and fled the scene on foot. In September, 1959, he was charged in

Sydney Central Criminal Court with 18 different offences, spread across 10 Sydney suburbs. He pleaded guilty without demur.

Detective Sergeant Brian Doyle, of the CID, said the crimes committed by Scanlon had serious, adverse effects, over a long period, on the lives of perhaps hundreds of thousands of people. A good number of the population of the areas in which Scanlon prowled were living in constant fear that he might strike at their homes. He added, in fairness to Scanlon, that because of publicity, the Police Department was flooded with frivolous calls, and many deliberate false reports of attacks. Some women even displayed cut-up clothing and inflicted minor self-injuries to their faces and breasts to give credence to their stories. Nevertheless, the feeling of fear in the suburbs had been real and justified.

At a sentencing hearing the next day, Mr Simon Isaacs, QC, appearing for Scanlon, addressed the question of his psychological state.

> What sort of individual is this person who lives a Jekyll and Hyde existence? He is a perfectly respectable and decent sort of citizen during the day, a good husband, and well regarded by his wife and employer. Yet he performs these strangely bizarre and sadistic acts at night.

> What sort of an individual is this person who takes such glee in not merely the doing of the act, but in leaving his imprimatur, enjoying the knowledge of the notoriety that has been created and the hunt that has ensued.

> Even in the absence of any evidence, one would not require any great exercise of intuitive thinking to conclude that this man is not all there. There is some

kink somewhere. This man is extremely abnormal. I put it to Your Honour that he, although sane, is nevertheless a sex-perverted psycho-neurotic, that he is mentally ill, and suffers a form of mental disease which has promoted him to commit these offences. Your Honour is dealing with an extremely abnormal individual, and the greater the degree of abnormality, the further you will get away from maximum penalties.

Mr Isaacs went on to suggest that Scanlon should thus be given three year's imprisonment, with the latter half of the term to be served on a prison farm while all the time being given psychiatric help. Mr Justice MacFarlane reserved his decision.

But one week later, the Justice made public his thoughts. He sentenced Scanlon to 18 years in gaol, with the hope that he might earn a remission of one-third if his conduct was satisfactory. If his response to treatment was adequate, then he might spend his later years on a prison farm. The Judge added that Scanlon had known what he was doing, and that what he was doing was wrong, and these two conditions together proved he was sane.

Scanlon appealed against the severity of the sentence on March 20 the following year. A panel of three judges rejected the appeal.

THE SPACE RACE

On September 13, there was good reason for Americans to walk about looking up into the sky, probably with their mouths open. The Russians had jumped way out in front in the Space Race, by launching a rocket that had entered into the lunar field of gravitation and was dead on course for the moon. This two-stage rocket weighed about one-and-a–half tons, and carried a vast range of scientific equipment. Most of the world was very impressed. For example, newspapers spoke of the feat in awe, and lavished praise on all concerned. The Manchester Guardian thought that "by any reckoning, the scientists and technicians who made the feat possible have proved themselves the Columbuses of the Space Age, and they deserve to be congratulated." The Vatican described the voyage as "a conquest for humanity." But there were a few people not so happy about it. The US State Department could only state that, in its opinion, "the Russians' feat yesterday of putting a hammer and sickle on the moon was no basis for a claim to sovereignty over the moon." US Vice President Nixon considered that there "was nothing to get excited about", and claimed that they had just recently failed in three previous attempts. However, he was not able to verify this in any way, and newspapers put his outburst down to "sour grapes."

The British Foreign Secretary, Selwyn Lloyd, debunked it all by saying "I doubt that many people are terribly interested in it." To which the Scotsman newspaper replied "it is a pity that in a first response to the Russian triumph, the American leadership and Selwyn Lloyd managed somehow to sound ingenuous, and at the same time, badly rattled."

The Sydney Morning Herald saw it as a fantastic and magnificent achievement. But, despite its enthusiasm for the future of space exploration, the Cold War caution was inevitably there.

The military implications of the Lunik can not be **burked**. It will still evoke an air of crisis in the Western capitals. For not only has Russia shown her capacity to shoot a rocket a quarter of a million miles, she has shown she can predict its time of arrival with an error of only 23 seconds. Such a degree of accuracy in cosmic rocketry carries the clearest terrestrial message for atomic warfare. The delicate balance of power has shifted in Russia's favour.

The Russians were not at all interested in **burking** on this issue. In fact, they rubbed salt into American wounds. On October 4th, they successfully sent off another rocket that by-passed the moon, and went around behind it, and was able to transmit pictures of the dark side back to earth for the first time. Apart from that, it left behind an "automatic interplanetary station" that we would now call a satellite. This was equipped with scientific and photographic equipment that continued to provide the Russians with lunar data for several months until the batteries ran out.

Comment. The Americans, over the last decade, had disparaged the Russians in their space efforts, and had convinced themselves that the US held an unbeatable lead. **Now**, they suddenly found that it was **they** who were behind. Two years later, when John Kennedy came to the Presidency, they went flat out to make up the difference, and by the end of the 1960's, they snatched the lead again, when they put men on the moon.

The Space Race still goes on, even today. At this moment, when some of the heat has gone out of the Communism versus Capitalism battle, there seems to be less urgency about who does what. But, the old rivalry is still there, and I expect it will flare up every now and then in the future.

But the propaganda value has now gone out of it. Back in 1959, either one of the two Great Powers, when it hit the lead, could say to the minnow nations of the world "We are well in front in space technology. Clearly that makes our economic system much better." Then, putting those two statements together, surely it followed logically that "In a war, we will clearly win, and so you had better join in with us." Curiously enough, such erudition did have a strong influence at the time, and it was this propaganda value of space feats that made them much more than scientific curiosities.

MR K AND MRS K IN THE USA

In late September, the international love-hate pendulum swung back again, and the Americans invited Nikita Khrushchev and his wife to visit the USA. Nikita accepted, and landed there at Washington Air Force base on September 16. The aim of the two Great Power leaders was to "melt the ice of the Cold War." A few hours earlier, the US Government had urged its citizens to be courteous rather than confrontative to the visiting party of 100, though Vice President Nixon urged them to be outspoken on controversial issues.

Khrushchev's itinerary took him to Washington and New York, where he was given an official motorcade though the streets. His reception from the people was eerily quiet, with no signs of the bunting and cheering that such occasions usually commanded. But given the large number of anti-Communist organisations in America, the absence of overt hostility was impressive. On September 20, he made a major speech to the United Nations. There, he called for the world to scrap all arms, but the West saw this as just propaganda, and the US Press saw it as "dull and old."

Feeling somewhat slighted, he then moved to Hollywood, where he got the first warm reception of his tour. At a luncheon given for him, his guests included Danny Kaye, Debohah Kerr, Ginger Rogers, Gary Cooper, Maurice Chevalier, Henry Fonda, Jean Simmons, Elizabeth Taylor, David Niven, Kim Novak, Marilyn Monroe, and Nat King Cole. Of course, all these actors had been through the persecution years of Senator Joe MacCarthy, and were thus less likely to be spooked by a Communist in their midst. He was well received by all the above.

Finally, he went to have two days of talks with President Eisenhower at Camp David, from which both parties emerged showing much satisfaction. Though it was noted that there were no specifics policies or initiatives announced.

Comment. It was all very lightweight. Mr K came across as a reasonable, yet cranky, person who knew his own mind. The President remained as aloof as possible from the day-to-day circus, and probably hoped that Mr K would make some terrible mistakes. But there was no harm done, and I'm sure that both men went home tired but happy. **But neither had changed in any way**.

Post Script. The American Press had been instructed by the Government not to attack Mr K while he was in the country. But they knew that his Communist ideology alienated him from the bulk of the American population, so they were happy to publish photos of him where he might look less than impressive. For example, they made a big show of him with a struggling turkey, and sure enough, he did not look **at all** impressive.

Further comment. For the last three Chapters, I have been expounding on the pervasiveness of the Cold War. For the rest of the book, I will give you a break, and scarcely mention it again. But, please remember, in the years round 1959, it was everywhere.

NEWS AND VIEWS

Frustrations. Every day, in my semi-retired stay-at-home life, I encounter all sorts of little frustrations that really get my goat. The morning newspaper is wrapped in cling plastic that I can't get off. The milk bottle has those green screw caps that won't budge, and then inside is another plastic wad permanently stuck to the mouth of the gadden. I can't open my Rice Bubbles without scissors. I can hear some type of noise coming from my neighbours. They call it music for an obscure silly reason. They now have adverts on SBS. And so on. It's a miracle that I survive.

There were also frustrations back in 1959. At times, they were so irritating that writers got some of it off their chests by writing to the Editors who, I am happy to say, have always found space for the such Letters, amidst the deadly tomes that come from politicians and pressure groups.

Letters, DISAPPOINTED MOTHER, Broken Hill. It would be timely and fair for the Department of Education to make it plain now to all those young ladies swotting hard for their Leaving Certificates that they must be only a minimum weight to obtain a **teacher-training scholarship.**

Many girls, potential teachers, put in a lot of time and study to secure a good LC pass, then find that they are overweight. The sedentary habit of five years in the classroom leads to a weight factor that debars a scholarship. A medico may supply a certificate that the applicant is in good health and without any disability other than the weight above the Department's maximum. It is then that the disappointed girl finds that she should have started her slimming along with her fifth year. There is not just time in the short period before the Leaving results and the Training Entrance medical exam to **reduce one's weight to the Department's stipulation**.

Therefore, if girls doing their LC look to their weight now and get it down in time to gain the 1960 scholarship, not so many would feel discouraged and disappointed. Most parents do not agree to a daughter going on reduced meals and doing a lot of exercise just when hard continued study needs extra resistance. Should these parents know of the keen disappointment they and their daughters will experience when it's too late, their attitude would possibly alter to a daughter's taking on weight reduction, slowly, now, under a doctor's guidance.

Comment. At the time, it was also true that applicants for scholarships would be **rejected if they were colour-blin**d.

Letters, K Hall. I would plead the cause of voluntary organizations which have hitherto depended on the Post Office for the dissemination of circulars among their members. **The proposed Postal Charges** appear to abolish the three pence halfpenny rate for circulars, which must in future go at five pence, whether sealed or not. This places a 43 per cent increase in cost on missionary and other religious organizations, P. and C. and Progress Associations, Trade Unions, cultural bodies and the like.

Letters, Mrs N Bloomfield, Trundle. As parents of a five-month-old infant, my husband and I are fully aware of the necessity of **vaccination against poliomyelitis**. It seems, however, that we, in common with many others, are to be penalised in this area by the **ineffective organization of the vaccination clinics**.

At the last clinic in Trundle, held on June 30, the serum had run out before we reached the head of the queue. As the clinic was next to proceed to Bogan Gate, 14 miles distant, we were ready to travel there if any serum was left over. Alas, there, too, there was not sufficient.

The following day, Friday, the clinic was to be held in Parkes. We were informed that "probably" there would be sufficient over to do any extras. Accordingly, we travelled 35 miles over a shocking road to that centre, to be informed upon arrival that there, too, they had run out.

Thus we have done everything possible to obtain the first injection for our baby, and the third for ourselves (having applied for and received the necessary cards) but to no avail.

Exhortations in the Press and over the air urging polio vaccinations are all very well for those able to receive them. What of people like ourselves who, having tried every means of obtaining these injections, fail because of the bungling of local government administration?

School uniforms. Uniforms were the exception, rather than the rule. Of course, in the richer private schools around the nation, they were compulsory. Also, at the major public High Schools in the bigger cities. In other High schools, and in primary schools, they were something of a rarity.

But, times were changing. I show a sample of correspondence of how parents felt about the increasing push for mandated uniforms.

Letters, Mary Shepherd. Wearing of a school uniform is, I have on good authority, not compulsory in Public Schools, and while education is compulsory I do not see how the uniform dressing of each and every child can be controlled. But it is a sad thing that pressure for uniforms is becoming far more than just subtle.

Earlier in the year at our local school the children were thundered at each morning to wear their uniforms. As a lone voice I protested to the headmaster and the pressure eased. Now I find the method thus: I am told by the children, "Mummy, I can't go to the folk-dancing unless I have a school uniform," and "Mum, can I go to see over State Parliament House and the Municipal Library. But I can't go unless I have the uniform." Apparently, the children of large families or the less-privileged of the community are to be debarred from these cultural pursuits.

I am very tired of being told how to dress my children by people who have no knowledge of my budget methods, nor of the specialised needs of this family. In other words, the schoolmaster is telling me how to spend my husband's hard-won earnings. Apparently, he does not approve of mother's industry in cutting down a coat to make a neat skirt for little Jeannie, or producing a pair of trousers for Johnny from dad's worn pants. Nor can mother go bargain-hunting and run up an 11-year-old's frock for 12 Shillings; no, she must simply wear her own clothes till they are shreds and yet contrive to appear bright and smart at all school functions, P. and C. meetings, fetes, etc., and, of course, produce donations for this and that on request. Remarkable people, mothers!

I am convinced secondary school is quite early enough for making children look just alike, conforming like rolled oats in a packet. I know all the arguments in favour of uniforms – the main one from the schoolteacher's viewpoint being that class discipline is made easier. Yes, naturally, those who look alike act alike – e.g., sheep – and regimentation of society follows easily. The trouble is, everything made easier for teachers makes difficulties for parents.

Letters, B Duval. Mary Shepherd has not, in my opinion, proved her case for the abolition of school uniforms. I feel she has overlooked a few facts.

Large families benefit from uniform clothing more than smaller ones. The life of a strong winter tunic is almost limitless. Hems go up and down, and seams are let out as the child grows; then they are handed down, and the seams come in and the hems go up again.

A summer tunic can be made, with less trouble than a frock, for twelve Shillings. Tunics are neater. The summer ones are easier to wash than frocks, and the winter ones are easy to home-clean. I can't see that children can be disciplined more easily in a uniform, but I do think uniforms assist the "parity of esteem," which is the ultimate aim of many of our clear-thinking educators.

Letters, Mother of four. I do not agree with Mrs Shepherd as I had two boys and two girls to dress on a very limited amount. It is far easier to dress boys and girls in uniform for school wear.

In two summer tunics, two for winter, and a change of blouses and jerseys, they were always tidy and neatly dressed. Many other children would go off in starched or faded dresses, clean on Monday, but not every day, and they look very different going home. The same for boys in tidy suits, which they changed when home from school. Appearance also makes pride, which I think is essential.

Obviously, after school uniforms, the next topic must be rusty steel wool. Here it is.

Letters, E King. Steel wool has been used for years in everybody's kitchen. For some years past, the Australian product has become useless on account of rust. Use it once and the next day it's just a lump of rust. The kind imported from the USA could be used indefinitely and was much cheaper than the local product.

Letters, Mrs I Hope. If your correspondent would go back to using soap instead of detergent for washing up, she would find that a pad of steel wool would last as long as any imported product. Detergent causes the rust, not the quality of the steel wool.

Letters, Miriam Blumenthal. If steel wool is rinsed and placed in a jar of clean water to which has been added one teaspoon of baking soda, it will not rust and will wear for a longer time than the imported product with more efficiency because it is much harder. I have had a pad in my kitchen sink for two weeks without rust appearing.

Letters, Anne Howard Toes. As a user of soap and not detergent, I still find that steel wool rusts very quickly indeed, wherever manufactured. Being dependent on tap water, and so not able to rinse steel-wool-scoured utensils properly, I have the greatest difficulty in not discolouring dishcloths and tea-towels used after it.

When I enquired of an engineer why steel wool could not be produced from stainless steel, he said that this would go into grit pieces and not fibre. What a boon it

would be if steel wool could be made stainless itself.
It would then be practically indestructible, and worth
any cost.

THE MASONS UNDER THE MICROSCOPE

The Masonic Lodge was a select body of Empire men who
for centuries had promoted themselves and good causes in
a secretive atmosphere. Entry to membership of the Lodge
was by invitation only, and its doings were tightly held
secrets. At the moment, in 1959, it was definitely on the
back-foot, and was at times being treated with contempt or
derision.

Recently it had suffered much bad publicity. I pick up
this story and examine correspondence that emanated with
Letters talking about how **the wives** of Members felt.

Letters, L E F. It is possible that, in leaving their
homes several times a week, they are making some
sacrifice on behalf of their fellow man. As far as I can
understand, Masonry is essentially a religion, and I
must admit that my husband, in common with many
others, had little or no thought for religion or religious
principles until he became a Mason. Surely this alone
is worthy of some sacrifice?

As for the festivities which usually follow the monthly
Masonic rites, has it not been established religious
tradition for centuries to partake of food and drink
with one's associates after a ceremony?

An analysis of the complaints of several of your
correspondents shows lack of understanding and
sympathy for the normal man's point of view, an
understanding which must, surely, be essential for a
successful and harmonious marriage.

Letters, Phoenix. I suggest she adopts the same
attitude to him **as one would to a child afflicted**

with an incurable disease. Any adult, be it man or woman, who has to seek the synthetic friendship of an organisation which is founded on the **childish practices** of secret signs and tawdry jewels superimposed on to odd bits of the Old Testament obviously needs love, care and understanding of his problem.

My husband has been a confirmed addict to Masonry for 35 years and is bound to numerous Chapters, holding many offices with grandiloquent titles. I seriously doubt if he has one genuine friend among the hundreds of acquaintances he has made over the years. The simulated heartiness of manner when Mason meets Brother Mason rings false to the perceptive ear. One hears of childish jealousies when a particular brother is elevated to a higher position in the hierarchy and is dubbed with a ridiculous title.

It is a matter for regret that so many men (and women), for they too have their particular craft, find it necessary to **bolster up their pitiful little egos with the drug known as Masonry**.

Letters, (Mrs) Mary Clements. At least Masons do have to come home to collect their little aprons and don their evening wear, have a hurried dinner and perhaps a word or two with members of their family - after all, half a loaf is better than nothing at all!

Since the beginning of time men - the really masculine, mentally alert, public-spirited and "good mixer" type of males - have always felt the compelling need for some sort of secret society, club, league or lodge where they can get a word in, sympathise, imbibe, eat, swap yarns and generally let their hair down without interference from yapping females, bawling kids and the icy blast of the mother-in-law's breath!

Naturally this promotes a better understanding, is good for business and gives a man a chance to fraternise, formulate ideas, compare notes and tune in on the general trend of politics, tribal or religious struggles, market values, sport, beer, etc. Since we are living in such a progressive and exciting period of history, men everywhere simply must draw closer together, know and fully understand what's going on beneath the surface, adopt wider and more tolerant views of the pressing international problems and cast aside parochialism and bigotry.

If Masonic Lodges help, then M P I and all the other long-suffering women who suffer in silence, as I have done for 40 years, are not keeping their tongues in their cheeks in vain!

Letters, Louise Rosenberg. The Masonic brotherhood seems to give its members self-confidence. It encourages an element of loyalty, at least among themselves; and if they possess even the smallest spark of moral integrity to begin with, it may help develop this. If there never was any, well, Freemasonry cannot make a man worse.

A dutiful wife will try to be patient, and not complain, looking for the improvement in her man. Should she herself find no pleasure in the social opportunities offered the wives, and does not feel dedicated to share her husband's interest, she may use her evenings alone to cultivate her own resources, to create worthwhile independent interests, so becoming a more integrated personality.

There is no need to begrudge a man this harmless pleasure. Three nights a week away from home in not unusual for a Mason who feels the need of something to boost his self-esteem or his manhood. It may seem excessive when a woman has become totally dependent on her husband's society.

OCTOBER: SIMMONDS, NEWCOMBE

News Reports, Monday, October 12, Sydney. Police Commissioner Delaney said this morning "two men have escaped from Sydney's Long Bay Gaol, and are at large in the community. They are both hardened criminals, and are known to be dangerous and should not be approached by members of the public. **They will not hesitate to kill.**

"The Government is offering a reward of 1,000 Pounds for information leading to their capture. Every available policeman in the State has been called in to watch for the fugitives."

The escape took place on Friday afternoon. On Sunday afternoon, a warder at Emu Plains Prison Farm was found brutally battered to death. The police were initially hesitant to link this crime to the two escapees, but subsequently, as they gathered more evidence, they became convinced that they were guilty. This added more to the pressure on police for early arrests.

The two escapees were Kevin Simmonds, aged 24, and Leslie Newcombe, aged 20. Police last night said that Simmonds was one of the most desperate criminals they had encountered in the last ten years. He had been serving a sentence of 15 years for armed hold-up when he escaped. In gaol he had boasted that he would soon escape, and that he would not be taken alive. He had a long history of crime including violence, and each time he was released from prison, he immediately plunged back into crime. Newcombe, before his escape, was serving three and a half years for breaking, entering and stealing, and was a well-behaved prisoner up to this point.

Over the next few weeks, the police search for the men was intensive and continuous. On the average day, police fielded about 500 calls per day In one typical hour, police checked reports that the escapees were on a Cremorne ferry, at Wynyard, at Dulwich Hill, at Marrackville, in a car at Wentworthville, and in a car at Drummoyne. Many of these calls were hoax calls, and many were from sympathisers with the convicts who were trying to slow the police down. On various days, the search moved out of Sydney, first towards Griffith, 400 miles South-East, where Simmonds' parents lived, then toward Dungog, 150 miles North On September 16, a milkman at Sydney's Mona Vale reported that a man who looked like Simmonds had approached, with a gun in his hand, and inter alia told him that "the police will never take me alive. I want you to pass that on to them."

Then on October 23, 14 days after their escape, police had a break-through. A young woman parked her car in Bondi, and went into a shop. When she came out, she saw the car was being driven off. She returned to the shop, and rang police, who set up road blocks. And at one of these, Newcombe was trapped and apprehended. He offered no resistance. His first words were "I'm glad it's all over. I'm pretty hungry." He had only three Shillings on him. Police intensified their activities in the area, but to no avail.

The next day, Newcombe was charged with having escaped from custody, the murder of the warder at Emu Plains, breaking into five shops, with stealing six cars. He made no plea; the whole process took two minutes. He said that for the first week of their freedom, he and Simmonds had hidden in the Showground, in a small makeshift cave they had constructed out of piled up bags of wheat. The entire Sydney Easter Show went on with them lying only a few feet away from the passing crowd. And while the military tattoo was on with the big crowds it attracted, they had remained in their cubby hole without emerging at all for three days. The pair had separated after a week.

So at the end of the month, Newcombe was back in custody, but Simmonds was well and truly on the loose. The police were a little wiser in that they were now sure that he was listening to their radio broadcasts, and was well aware of many of their moves. We will catch up with him next month.

OBITUARIES

In a remarkable few weeks from mid-October, **three** well-known men died untimely deaths.

The first of these, **Mario Lanza,** was an American tenor, who thrilled Australian audiences in musicals such as *That Midnight Kiss, The Toast of New Orleans, The Great Caruso,* and *Because You're Mine.*

Lanza died at the early age of 38, from a coronary embolism, following double pneumonia.

The second was Sydney and national radio and television personality, **Jack Davey.** He was host to breakfast shows emanating from Melbourne and Sydney. From the 1930s to the 1950s, his shows were distinguished by his hearty sign-on call of "High Ho, Everybody, This Is Jack Davey" In the 1950s, he was applauded for compering the Ampol Show, and the widely successful quiz show *GIVE IT A GO.*

Such was his popularity that his funeral attracted a crowd of 125,000 people.

The third was **Errol Flynn**. This cavalier Tasmanian had a very distinguished father who was quite famous for his pioneering work with a variety of native animals. Errol, however, was not so distinguished as a scholar, and was asked to leave several Primary Schools. When he came to Sydney, he was expelled from Sydney Grammar School. As a young man he took off on a yacht to New Guinea, and spent some time there before he was discovered as an actor, and proceeded gradually to Hollywood.

There, in the later 1930's and early 1940's, he acted in movies such as *Captain Hawk, Robin Hood, and Dawn Patrol.*

He was an athletic handsome devil, and became famous for his swashbuckling roles and for his physical prowress. He was apparently also very successful with the ladies off-screen, and indeed his fame as a ladies' man is now legendary.

Comment. As a young lad, I saw him in all of those movies. I was not conscious of his good looks, but his great feats of derring-do thrilled me to the core, and filled dreamy nights of my childhood with images of myself doing such wonderful and righteous deeds. He was a hero to end all heroes, and not even Harrison Ford has come near to surpassing him.

CURE FOR CANCER.

By the end of the 1950's, cancer in Australia was just starting to get some publicity. Prior to this period, it was a hush-hush disease, not spoken about. To say that a person had cancer was generally considered as saying that he was going to die soon. Along with this attitude came the acceptance that there was no **cause** for cancer. A lot of people thought that cancer just came randomly to certain unfortunates, and another group thought that it was inherited so that if your father "had" it, **you too** were likely. But the idea that foreign, toxic substances were a **cause** was just not thought of. So that meant that the idea of taking evasive action was just not thought of. There was no talk **then** of giving up smoking because of the risk of cancer. Don't be silly.

Of course, overseas in the US and Britain, the large tobacco processors were growing more aware of the links to tobacco. They had already taken a few desultory measures against smokers quitting if the link proved to be true, and if it became known and appreciated. But in the meantime, back here in the colonies, existing adult male smokers rolled-their-own and puffed away contentedly, while at the same time, females and ever-younger youths joined their ranks.

The two items below, dated 1959, show just the very beginning of the realisation that toxic substances, not just tobacco, and situations, were high on the list of causes. As you read them, you should recognise that many readers at the time thought that most statements in them were rubbish. Indeed, as you read the second item you might come to that conclusion yourself.   It has taken another 50 years almost for society to come to a cause-and-effect model, with a dash of heredity thrown in.

Press release, Committee against Smoking. The visit of Professor Jethro Gough has again highlighted the danger of lung cancer caused by smoking.

One is not surprised that such sporadic reminders make little impression on the smoking public, in view of the enormous extent of psychology-based advertising by tobacco companies. This is designed to build a favourable mental association of smoking with poise, dignity, attractiveness, and tranquility, thus to maintain popular demand through unconscious motivation, now specially directed to capture the teenage and female market.

Almost 1,600 lung-cancer deaths occurred in 1957 in Australia. This represents many thousands of skilled man-hours lost to our economy while the Government seeks immigrants to build a stronger nation based on adequate population.

The authorities should, surely, aim to reduce this human waste – perhaps, as one Scandinavian country has done, not by restricting sales or availability, but by limiting advertising of tobacco products. Thus, while permitting the whole freedom to indulge, it assists the public health by reducing the tobacconists' advertising and thus the psychological impetus towards smoking.

Fortunes are spent in saving the newborn. How much more valuable is the trained and experienced middle-aged citizen, now exposed by his smoking habit to the danger of lung cancer. Are we to ignore the peril to future generations of the systematic indoctrination of youth by the psychologists of the tobacco companies?

Letters, J Pope. I was particularly interested to note that the Commonwealth and the States were going to investigate the use of various lipstick colouring substances in relation to the possible incidence of cancer.

May I suggest that these custodians of the public health carry their studies a little further and ascertain the extent to which such troubles may be aggravated by the almost universal use today of synthetic (non-soap) wetting agents in toothpastes.

The degreasing potency of these are well known and the daily use of dentifrice containing them by persons as young as the kindergarten child must remove the natural protective skin oils, leaving the lips an easy victim to the actinic rays of the sun, which are so closely associated with the all-too-frequent skin cancer of today.

There appears to be an urgent need for a very full and independent study, a survey of dentifrice manufacturers' research, and a request for information from the US Food and Drug Administration to be made by these public officers in the interest of the young children of today in particular, and the people in general.

CONCERN FOR YOUNG WOMEN

News Item. Federal Council of Roman Catholic Women. At the annual meeting, a delegate, Mrs L Quinn, expressed her worries about the dire fate that awaited many young women.

She asked mothers to discourage the children from following the slavish dictates of so-called fashion. She pointed out the evil associated with lack of decency among young girls and intoxicating liquor. She warned that alcohol was being drunk in lounges, clubs, and at pre-ball parties. Also, she regretted, in some private homes.

She went on to say that great vigilance on the part of parents should be exercised. This vigilance should be exercised irrespective of the types of homes in which the parties are held. All too often they lead to the first steps away from sobriety, dignity, and modesty. Urged on by unscrupulous people, they engendered a false sense of enjoyment and adventure which ultimately may lead to downfall and disgrace.

NO GAOL FOR HP DEFAULTERS

Over the last decade, Hire Purchase had revolutionised personal finance. Put simply, it meant that a family could buy something now, and pay for it later. Before HP came along, people had to save the money first.

The main items bought on HP were motor cars, and the boom toy of the fifties, television sets. But along with the glee of early purchases came the pain of having to pay for them. Some people fell behind in their payments, and in many States, this meant Court proceedings, and often gaol for defaulters.

On September 1st, the NSW Attorney-General announced that such a penalty would no longer be enforceable. This had been agreed at an all-States conference on HP provisions, and drafting of the uniform legislation would be commenced forthwith. Instead of a gaol term, a maximum fine of 200 Pounds would be substituted.

COLOUR BAR IN SPORT

In 1959, South Africa, and also New Zealand to a lesser extent, were opposed to having blacks play sports with whites. In South Africa, apartheid was well entrenched and no South African black could get a jersey in any National team. In New Zealand, this policy was not so well entrenched, but a team going to South Africa could not give offence to the South Africans by including blacks.

I enclose a Letter that reminds you of small that the colour bar was still alive and well, but that opposition to it was growing. .

Letter, Polland OReagen, Citizens' All Black Tour Association, New Zealand. The decision of the NZ Football Union to exclude Maori players from selection for the NZ Rugby team to tour South Africa has met with criticism from a wide and substantial cross-section of people throughout New Zealand. We who are endeavouring to organise sufficient public opinion to right the present situation are anxious that people overseas should know that opposition is growing daily and every effort is being made to have the decision of the Rugby Union reversed.

TOO OLD AT 70?

Letters, W B Donnolley. With the approach of the local government elections, it is appropriate that the community should reflect upon the efficiency of councils and those elected to serve on them.

Under our system, where men and women are obliged to offer their services in a voluntary capacity, it does not appear always possible to attract the most efficient people to office. During the past two years I have had the opportunity of examining at first hand the activities of councils throughout the State and of meeting many who served on them.

I formed the opinion, and I know this is shared by many in local government, that one of the greatest problems is the army of elderly men who are well entrenched, and who refuse to give up what has developed into an interesting social life. Many of these men are retired and can afford to devote long hours to this pastime. But are they giving efficient service?

Local government nowadays is big business, with annual incomes exceeding 1 million Pounds. Surely the functions of councils - municipal, shire and county - should be in the hands of clear-thinking, energetic and efficient people.

There are may, including myself, who would like to see a compulsory retiring age of 70 introduced. After all, this age limit applies to hospital boards, land boards, and a variety of trusteeships.

NAMING YOUR SUBURB OR TOWN

Letters, A Chisholm, President, Royal Australian Historical Society. Members of my Society, who have long been concerned with the place-names of this country, deplore the recent upsurge of terms that are merely vulgar, cheap, exotic, or all three.

Following a discussion by my Council some weeks ago, it was resolved to explore the possibility of creating an organised body that would foster a more enlightened approach to place-naming in future sub-divisions etc., and perhaps offer help in finding suitable names.

Accordingly, we are interested to learn that an official of the Australian National Travel Association, newly returned from abroad, has revealed that the use of American place-names in Australia is regarded as being "stupid." So, of course, it is, and the Americans are quite justified in asking why Australia favours "tinselly" borrowings when home-grown names are available.

The worst centre of this fatuous practice, Surfers' Paradise, is probably beyond saving, but some attempt should be made, as a matter of national pride and in the interests of tourism, to prevent the blight from spreading.

It is therefore to be hoped that the relevant authorities, including the Local Government Association and the Real Estate Institute, will realise that a helpful measure of control of place-naming, beginning with estate development, is highly desirable.

NEWS AND VIEWS

Scotch back on shelves. The Federal Government's recent easing of import restrictions means that drinkers will be able to buy bottles of whisky from hotels and clubs **for consumption in their our homes**. Since early in the War, this has not been possible. For about the last decade, whisky could be bought by the noggin over the counter, but it was not available to buy by the bottle and take away. That situation is now reverted to what is hoped to be normal.

Currency. Letters, J Swift. It is to be fervently hoped that Harold Holt has already commissioned numismatologists to study the question of the re-introduction of **the groat** to the national currency.

I am compelled to wander the landscape burdened with a coin bag in my hip-pocket holding at least 24 pieces of bronze ironmongery, weighing eight ounces, to pay for the half-dozen telephone calls incidental to my business. The circulation of the fourpenny piece would relieve an intolerable situation.

Hitch-hikers. Letters, Betty Howard, Yass. You recent corespondent talked about how motorists should be wary of picking up "unknown characters" thumbing a lift. As a regular driver along country roads, I have had the pleasure and privilege of helping along the road innumerable characters: teenage boys and girls full of adventure and wanting to see all they can of their own country for as little as they can; semi-trailer drivers stranded because they are broken down;

shearers who want to get to their next shed, and who have missed out on legitimate transport; and, in one case on the Pacific Highway, a railway man who had to travel about 20 miles and but for the lift would have had to waste a whole Saturday morning.

You get a glimpse into the lives of these people as you drive along. You hear their philosophies. My own philosophy is that I am extremely lucky to own a car at all, and I'm glad to share it with other wayfarers.

Mail deliveries. Letters, Joy Wallace. I am appalled at the suggestion that, for economy's sake, the afternoon delivery of mail in the suburbs should be discontinued. The aim should be to improve facilities and services in the nation where the population is increasing. The mails are slow enough here, heaven knows, without making them any worse

In England, (I am an Australian), one can post a letter up to 6 pm in London's suburbs and it will be delivered by 9 next morning as far afield as a tiny village in Cornwell or Glasgow or Edinburgh. Also, in London's suburbs, there are up to four deliveries a day, and even three in Hertfordshire villages.

Comment. In Australia, in 2016, you can post an **Express Post** letter at 6.01pm on Friday, and it won't get **cleared from the box** until 6pm on Monday. **That's service for you.**

NOVEMBER: NO PICNIC IN THE BUSH

Simmonds on the run. On November 6, two park rangers were driving through Kur-ring-gai Park, a very large bushland to the North of Sydney. They noticed that, off-track, sand was being shovelled, and stopped to see what damage was being done. They saw a man there digging with a long-handled shovel. One of the two men, Colin Green, said "I am a ranger, what do you think you are doing?" To which the digger answered, as he picked up a .38 revolver "I am Simmonds." The ranger replied "I don't care who you are, you can't go digging up the dirt." Simmonds told them that "you have put me in a very difficult situation. I do not know what to do with you."

What he reluctantly decided to do was to tie them up, leave the cubby hole, and take their ute to move on elsewhere. He forced the two men at gunpoint to tie each other up, and then took his leave. He was with the two captives for about half an hour. Green later said "I was scared only twice. The first time was when Simmonds pointed the gun at us. The second time was when he was leaving. He got in the truck, and then came back. I had a fair idea that he was going to do us in. But he just wanted to get his road map from the stolen car nearby in the bushes."

The two men quickly untied each other, ran hundreds of metres to a bitumen road, hailed a passing motorist, got to a phone box, and telephoned police. Road blocks and searches and police dogs were mobilised.

Their efforts almost bore fruit. Just before dawn, two police officers who had set up a roadblock near Wyong Bridge were startled by a car coming through without stopping, at seventy miles an hour. One of them, a young Constable Hayward, recognised Simmons, and gave chase on his motor bike.

Simmons turned off onto bush tracks, and going now at eighty miles an hour, got into some mud, and ran off the road. He scurried into the bush, with the Constable hot on his heels. He turned and pointed his gun, and said "Stop. I'm warning you, copper" and disappeared into thick shrub. The Constable fired two shots into the thicket, but to no avail. One again, the alarm was raised, and the police were getting closer.

Newspapers reported next day that police now believed that "Simmons is on Jilliby Ridge, a heavily timbered wilderness, near the bush city of Wyong, 60 miles from Sydney. It rises five hundred feet out of a plain, and is about five miles long. It is notorious for its infestations of leeches and ticks, and thick with wild cats and snakes. Simmonds, dressed only in shorts and a singlet, would be well advised not to eat the berries, because they were certain to poison him."

But "Houdini-like", he slipped out of the cordon that had been set up round the ridge, and he went into Jilliby Valley. There, he broke into an empty farmhouse, rested for half an hour, had a feed of raisins, and listened to news broadcasts on the radio. He left with a blanket, a groundsheet, and food.

By now, Sunday, there was a police constable in every farmhouse in the Wyong area. Road traffic back to Sydney was delayed for several hours for motorists who had to pass through three road blocks and have their cars searched each time. Then on Sunday evening, police found Simmonds' barefoot tracks on a bush-path, and called in the dogs. The dogs relished their task, and with ever-increasing enthusiasm, bounded towards the capture. But, the elements were not on their side. A huge thunderstorm hit the area, and washed out all smells and tracks. So, by that Sunday night, he was still free.

For the next week, the search went on. Every train going through Wyong, on the main line to Brisbane, was searched. Boats on nearby Lake Macquarie were picketed to stop an escape by sea. But the barefoot and footsore Simmonds was now nowhere to be seen. Was he even still in the area?

Well, yes and no. On Saturday evening, he was sighted by a few people near Mulbring, twenty miles north of Wyong. He was again pursued by police dogs, but they lost the scent when he detoured into a creek and swam for 500 yards along it, Then he stumbled eight miles to Kurri Kurri. There, he stole a car, but it ran out of petrol. By now he was in Kurri township, and so too were several hundred police. He used the thick fog to hide in a thick clump of bush but, for a third time, the police dogs picked up his scent. Four officers of the law, with guns drawn, moved through the scrub to where a few horses were looking at something behind a tree. They then saw Simmonds, and at the same time, he saw them. He walked from behind the tree, with his hands up, and while one Detective Ray Kelly held him, another handcuffed him.

Post Script. Simmonds, during his 37 days at large, became something of a folk hero. He was intelligent, quite handsome and, time and again, slipped through the lines of

500 police with all the legendary skill and guile of a Robin Hood. So as he went along in that period, several fan clubs were started in Sydney. When he was captured in Kurri, 500 local citizens, mainly women, got up early to see him enter the police station there. Several women said, "Oh, the poor thing" and "isn't it a shame." When one woman in the crowd said "Good on you, Kevin", his face lit up and he gave her a smile.

He was also on good terms with the police. On the car trip from Kurri to the gaol at the small bush city of Wyong, he was given nine big sandwiches, a quarter of a pound of chocolate, an apple, and six biscuits. Then for lunch, at Wyong police station and gaol, he had lamb chops, chocolate cake, several pints of milk, and tea. The clean clothing and extra food were given to him by detectives who "chipped in." In the evening, he had a baked dinner, prepared by the station sergeant's wife, and at 9 o'clock, he was allowed to go to sleep.

His good treatment however, did not last. In December, trial proceedings against him and Newcombe were initiated, and continued in the New Year. They were charged with murder, but were found guilty of manslaughter. The judge obviously though they should have been found guilty of the murder charge, and sentenced them to life imprisonment, to be served at the notoriously tough Grafton Prison. Once there, Simmonds found prison life unbearable, and deteriorated quickly to the stage where he hanged himself in November, 1967.

A NEW GOVERNOR GENERAL

The popular Sir William Slim had served his six-year term in Australia, and so he went his merry way back to England. Our Prime Minister, over the dead bodies of the Labor Party, once again ignored Australian replacements, and appointed the ex-Speaker of the House of Commons as the Governor General. His given name was Shepherd Morrison, and he answered to that until he left the House. But at that stage, as was customary for a retired Speaker, he was given the title of Viscount Dunrossil, of Vallaquie in the Isle of North Uist and County of Inverness. Despite this load, he was the heir apparent to William Slim, after he relinquished the post

Unfortunately, the Viscount made a little bit of history in this nation. He became the first Governor General to die in office, after holding the position for barely a year.

THE QUEEN'S ENGLISH

One of the good things about coming to November each year is that about halfway through the month, most of the bad and scary news, reported in the newspapers, dries up. The proprietors of the various media outlets realise that at that time, **readers turn into Christmas shoppers**, and don't want to be scared and worried by all the fears and scandals that the newspapers and others feed them for most of the year.

So, the pages are filled with adverts, and good cheer stories. But, as another by-product, they open up their Letters pages to all sorts of comments and controversies, most of them delightful for their sheer superficiality, that at other times of the year are buried.

Below, we have a few Letters that were written in the Christmas spirit. At the end, they do not prove a lot, but surely we can afford a few luxuries at this time of the year.

Letters, DISGUSTED. There is great and urgent need for a united effort to suppress the prevalent and ugly mutilation of the English language resulting from the use of genteelisms. I refer in particular to the vulgar and increasingly common use of the word "toilet", which is apparently regarded by the ignorant or genteel as a suitable euphemism for the water closet.

The word "toilet" originally signified a small cloth to cover the dressing table, and is now properly applied to the mode or operations of dressing. Its misuse above mentioned receives no support from such authorities as the Shorter Oxford English Dictionary, Chamber's Dictionary, Roget's Thesaurus and Fowler's Modern English Usage.

There are several perfectly satisfactory words for the place thus misnamed. My own preference is for the succinct word "privy", but "water closet" and its abbreviation "WC", also "latrine", are all equally lucid. The euphemism "lavatory", despite the support of popular and moderately established usage, is better avoided so long as architects and members of the building trade still use this word in its correct sense. Perhaps it is not too much to expect that they may eventually teach others to do the same.

Letters, B Foggon. All lovers of the English language, pure and undefiled, must agree with recent statements about the harm that is being done by genteelisms. One of the worst of these is the use of the word "lady" when referring to women generally, and not to a particular type of woman. This has reached the stage of absurdity when we see on the doors in city buildings "men" and on other doors in the same building "ladies."

Almost as bad is the growing pretentiousness, so that a thing is never completed or concluded but "finalised", and never happens or occurs but "transpires", a horrid word which in any case means "to become known."

Letters, Grace Tully. Modern commercial advertising is responsible for the introduction of a large number of terms which attempt to remove the suggestion of social inferiority attaching to the ordinary word for the thing mentioned. A boarding house becomes a "guest-house", and a boarder or lodger a "paying guest." In the more genteel districts, property is not sold; it is "disposed of."

People who would hate to be caught buying a cheap article allow themselves to be attracted by something "inexpensive". Again, in times more squeamish that our own, certain people thought it desirable to replace unpleasant, downright words like "spit", and "sweat", by "expectorate" and "perspire". The trouble is, however, that all these polite synonyms in time acquire the same associations as the original words, so that we might as well be content to call a spade a spade.

Letters, Claude McKay. I suffered agonies when I was a young reporter on Sydney's "Evening News." The editor would not permit anything to happen or occur. Whatever it was or by what means it came about, it had to transpire. I had long ago despaired of ever making a policeman go anywhere in the paper. He always "proceeded."

One day, I read a short story in the "Strand Magazine." It was written by Morley Roberts, and in the central part he told of the arrival on the scene of "a second rate reporter, transpiring at every pore." As it was a newspaper story, I gave it to my sub-editor to read. Thereafter, he blue-pencilled the detestable word.

Letters, V Bray. Your correspondents have not mentioned "New Australians." This is a phrase coined by the Department of Immigration public relations officers, and it gives offence to hundreds of thousands of people. Most of the "New Australians" I have met would prefer the frank, good-natured term of "foreigners" to this genteelism, which they regard as a patronising way of talking about second-class citizens. This has filtered through to Immigration officials who are now showing a deplorable tendency to use instead "New Settler" or even "New Citizen." Why not stick to the plain, established term "migrant.". Or even go back to the pre-War term of "reffo." Or even, what they were generally called then, "bloody reffo."

SNAKES ALIVE AND DEAD

I suppose you might say that the next topic fits the bill I described above. That is, it is undoubtedly superficial. I do not argue with that. But I add that when I come to select the Letters I will include in my books, I go to small groups of older citizens, who tell me which of them they would include. When I came to the next topic, these wise men and women were unanimous that the Letters on snakes were of universal appeal to Australians, and should definitely be included. So, I bow to their wisdom and here they are.

Letters, G Southern. I read in your columns that there were three acceptable methods of killing a snake. First, chop its head off with a long-handled shovel. Second, whip it across the neck or back with a length of flexible fencing wire. Third, best of all, shoot it with a shotgun. But the first and third of these methods are dangerous. And, far from being the best of all, a shotgun is the most dangerous.

A long-handled shovel is indeed an ideal weapon, properly used. But the silliest thing to do with it is chop the snake's head off; for a snake's head, separated from its body, can still travel at speed, and can bite. I have seen a snake's head kill a dog in that way.

The right way to use a long-handled shovel is simply to chop the snake, anywhere along the body, for a start, so as to break its back, but without severing it. Once its back is broken, the snake cannot travel, and it is then a simple matter to crush its head with the edge of a shovel.

The shotgun is dangerous precisely because, at close range, unless it shatters the snake's head with a direct hit, it is likely to sever the head from the body. That leaves the head free to travel and bite. An ordinary .22, especially if it is a repeater, is a much safer weapon to use. If you miss the snake's head and hit it elsewhere, there is no risk of a single hit cutting the snake in two.

It is as well to remember that the snake, when its body is extended, can, by raising its head, strike forwards, or even backwards; but it cannot strike sideways to the alignment of its body on the ground. When approaching it with a suitable weapon, it is wise, therefore, to keep to one side of it.

Letters, Roy Mackay, Australian Herpetological Society. Mr Southern's statement that the severed head of a snake can still live to bite is quite incorrect – physically. This story, and the one about the snake swallowing its young, for protection, are so much part of those perpetual yarns of the Australian bush lore. And for that matter, these stories arose from similar stories from other lands.

Whether the head is severed or merely has its head crushed makes no difference; the snake is dead. However, as with most snake yarns, there is a core of sound fact. The nerves of such a snake are apt to make its body squirm and wriggle for some time afterwards. Certainly, if one puts one's finger into the mouth of such a mortally wounded snake, the reflex action of the nerves may close upon the digit and inject venom. But who is going to do that?

Nevertheless, whether the snake is killed by shovel or shot, it will be officially dead and cannot physically or consciously continue on its way to seek out prey or its would-be slayer.

Letters, A Mathews. Roy Mackay seems a little too dogmatic about severed snakes being "officially" dead. I seem to have read long ago about someone being bitten by a snake's head which flew off during a whip-cracking exhibition and struck his toe; and a personal experience of my own nearly thirty years ago is worth recounting.

Digging for rabbits with a mattock on the edge of a small blackberry bush near Crookwell, I disturbed a black snake about two feet long, and struck it with a mattock, cutting it neatly in two. No doubt the front section was a little longer than the other, but there must have been at least one third of the total length, or I would not have been so astounded by what followed, or retained such a vivid memory of it.

As I attempted to strike again with the clumsy mattock, the business end of the snake, with head raised, wriggled into the blackberries. As I scratched round with the mattock to drag it out again, it wriggled round a small circle (about 18 inches in diameter) and emerged close to my feet and near its still-squirming tail, which of course had not moved from where it was severed. Coming upon this detached portion of its own body, the snake, travelling all the time with its head raise, struck viciously at it. The ill-treated tail section gave one convulsive jerk as it was struck, and lay still. Another blow of the mattock then end of the story.

Mr Mackay may find this hard to believe. I suggest that if he wants to make authoritative statements in these things he should make some practical experiments to find out the minimum proportion of a snake's length that can retain death-dealing vitality and let your readers know the results.

Letters, Grace Clayton. To recent Letters remind me of the time I pulled up a biggish eel when fishing from a jetty in Tasmania. To kill the eel seemed quite okay at the time. I lashed the eel a few times on the jetty until it lay quite still, and cut off its head with my sharp fishing knife.

Now the problem was to retrieve my hook, which seemed to be embedded in the creature's mouth. I put out my hand to pick up the dead fish, and got the shock of my life. The head sprang at me and got my left thumb between its teeth, piercing the nail. And then my arm fell off.

CENSORSHIP NOT IN WARTIME

Every year since the War, there had been strong criticism of the enforcement of censorship rules in Australia. In 1959, this remained in chaos. It was carried out at two levels. **Firstly, the Commonwealth** had its say, and exercised its authority over imports of books through its Customs Department. **Then the States** each had their own system, and they normally operated under the all-seeing eye of a sergeant of Police, and who would be well equipped to direct traffic. The justification for using such sergeants was that they were **not** experts in literature, but ordinary citizens, and it was **their** interests that were being protected.

In both cases, the restrictions imposed were heavy-handed, ignorant, and capricious, and attracted regular criticism from the Editors of all the daily papers. The review below summarises what the Sydney Morning Herald thought of things now.

The Editor of the *SMH* became incensed at the level of censorship being foisted on the community. He pointed out that love scenes from one of the highest rated films of the year "Room at the Top" had been lacerated to protect us "from the impact of physical passion." He pointed out that Lolita, a book widely discussed right around the world for all this decade was still banned here. So too was Brenden Behan's own story of life in prison, "Borstal Boy." "So great is the power of our censors in the Customs Department, that the publishers of Norman Lindsay's "Redheap" have decided to publish a watered-down version for Australia."

The general theme behind this censorship is that Australia is not mature enough to appreciate adult themes. The level of blame stretches from the officials involved, the politicians who cringe from making controversial decisions, to the readers themselves who are servile in the face of this official oppression. He concludes with a call for a "critical review of the entire outdated concept that we need protecting at all, and that we cannot be trusted to use our own judgement.

A response. As usual, someone out there thought differently, and was not shy about putting his point of view on paper.

Letters, Neil McQueen. I am very sorry to see the SMH lower its level by publishing your opinions on censorship. I confess I have not read much pornography. I read a little of "Borstal Boy" and found it intolerably dull and unpleasant, and also some of Lindsay's work.

No doubt I am one of those with "primitive views on art and morals", but in my profession we see the result of brutal passion to such an extent that we would like our young people to grow up with a healthy attitude towards life and not to have their minds assailed by descriptions of animal obscenities masquerading under the title of art.

As one with some pretence to knowledge of practical psychology, I should judge that you have some very indigestible inhibitions which probably will not, at this stage, respond to treatment. But we "wowsers" object to the exposure of the minds of our future citizens to beastliness which can be just as harmful as cocaine and heroin, from which most of us believe they should be protected. I am, in fact, one of "the wowsers who know not better."

ABORIGINES AND LIQUOR

Letters, I Commons. Still another Aboriginal in trouble, through a white man (with a black heart) selling him liquor. It is the evil white man, to my mind, who should be imprisoned for supplying the liquor.

I have seen publicans in the country putting two or three bottles of beer through a paling fence, for an Aboriginal waiting outside, and the gap closed again. Those are the men to punish.

All my life I have known the poor old Aboriginal, as servants and men working on the property. A splendid, kindly, clever people, and I feel nothing but anger and indignation for the law that can treat them so unjustly.

They have their own strict laws, but few white people have ever taken the trouble to find out. I have often wondered why the Government cannot train these young lads, in the same way as the white boys are trained as Army cadets. It would be so good for them.

But I am 92 years of age and rather old for this kind of thing and the world has changed since the bushranger days. This may not be of much interest to you, but to me it is. Perhaps I feel too indignant.

NEWS AND VIEWS

Letters, Don Richards. I was very pleased to read that the US Food and Drug Administration has banned the use of 17 coal-tar colours in the manufacture of lipsticks, and that this ban threatens the very existence of the American lipstick industry. However, it is a sad commentary on mankind if the demise of this barbaric custom of painting one's face were the result of imposed health regulations, rather than a voluntary rejection.

BANKS ARE EVERYWHERE

One noticeable feature of these times is the high number of banking-type branches present in all suburbs and regional centres. Every financial organisation, from the big ones to the tin-pots, have a branch in the High Street, and some have two within a few hundred metres of each other.

Over the next decade, the number reduced as takeover fever got a foothold and the industry was rationalised.

DECEMBER: 10 HIT SONGS FROM AMERICA

If	Perry Como
Be My Love	Mario Lanza
Too Young	Nat King Cole
Come On-a My House	Rosemary Clooney
Cold, Cold Heart	Tony Bennett
Cry	Johnny Ray
Gone Fishin'	Bing Crosby
Jezabel	Frankie Laine
Rose, Rose, I Love You	Frankie Laine
My Heart Cries For You	Dinah Shore

10 MOVIES RELEASED

Show Boat	Katherine Grayson
An American in Paris	Gene Kelly
A Streetcar Named Desire	Leigh and Brando
Place in the Sun	Elizabeth Taylor
Quo Vadis	Taylor and Kerr
African Queen	Bogart, Hepburn
Born Yesterday	Judy Holliday
Comin' Round the Mountain	Abbott and Costello
Strangers on a Train	Farley Grainger
Lavender Hill Mob	Alec Guinness

ACADEMY AWARDS

Best Actor, Humphrey Bogart (African Queen)

Best Actress, Vivien Leigh (A Streetcar Named Desire)

DRINK DRIVING TESTS?

In 2016, no matter which State we live in, we all accept the idea that police have the right to breath-test us for alcohol as part of random testing, or after an accident. This was not always the case. In 1959, the idea, world-wide, was fairly new, and in Australia was tentatively gaining support in some sections of the community and in the legislatures.

At that time, random testing as well as booze buses were unheard of. Generally, testing for alcohol was restricted to drivers **who requested it after an accident.** And the reason they would do that was to show later to a court that they were **not** drunk at the time of their accident. The police had no power to compel a person to take a test. And where a test was taken, a **doctor** had to be called, and he had to be prepared to come to the site of the accident. There were all sorts of variations on this general description, as you will see from the following papers on the subject. You will also see that it was a hot topic, and I should tell you that discussions of the subject went on from here for years, and in fact, decades.

Press report, A Rylah, Chief Secretary, Victoria.
Mr Rylah said that he had just received a report from Dr K Bowden, the Government pathologist, who is abroad studying road toll problems for the State. He had visited a number of European nations, and had found that they varied a great deal in their handling of drunk drivers. For example, in Sweden and Germany, roadblocks were used to intercept random drivers, who were given compulsory tests on the spot. In Sweden, results of the tests, done by doctors and **chemists**, were accepted by the Courts, and there was no need for them to go to Court to give evidence. If the driver

was found to not have effective control his vehicle, the public had realised that his licence was automatically suspended, and he was sent to gaol for one to three months.

In Sweden, after 33 years of compulsory blood tests, compulsion was still part of the law, but the public had matured in its attitude, and was now largely self-regulating. That is, many heavy drinkers leave their cars and go home by taxi or foot.

When we look back in 2016 such opinions were not surprising. But it came as a shock to Australians in 1959 to find that **compulsory testing had been in force** in parts of Europe for some time, and that people could be sent to gaol. Also, it was accepted practice here that only a doctor could administer the tests, and for us to find that a chemist was being used overseas started some people thinking. They started to realise that the oft-quoted argument, **that random testing could not be done because of a shortage of doctors, perhaps did not hold up.** Now, their argument became that chemists could be used, and from there it was a short step to nurses, and ultimately to policemen. In any case, despite the Season of Good Cheer being upon us, Letters flowed in at a fast rate. In fact, the last one quoted here was published on December 28th.

Letters, F Hanesman, Macquarie Street, Sydney.
Mr Rylah's report mentioned the possibility of errors arising in administration of a blood test. I contend it is almost inconceivable that an innocent person would suffer an injustice because of such an event.

The rest of the report indicates that the countries referred to appreciate the value of having blood tests. Opposition to these in this country stems from obstinacy, ignorance or vested interest and an indifference to the value of human life.

Blood tests are always found to be a deterrent. That is the purpose of our agitation for their introduction. Let us cut out red herrings, and do something realistic to effect reduction in the toll of the road.

Letters, L Howell. One of your correspondents, Dr L Norman, is of the opinion that blood testing is "desirable but impracticable". I agree with him.

I would like to see Dr Hanesman prove just how compulsory blood tests can be put into practical operation throughout the State at all hours for all accidents. That's what compulsory means. If he can, we might get somewhere. So far, only a very small minority of countries and some of the United States use the method.

Letters, F Hanesman, Macquarie Street, Sydney. Mr L Howell's Letter makes me sad. I know his great interest in road safety, and I did not expect him to raise another red herring. Of course it is impracticable to have a 24-hour service throughout the State for the purpose of taking blood. But we did not wait till we were able to provide such a service for police patrols, ambulances, telephone service or any other essential service and we still have not attained that ideal.

In Brisbane some 90 per cent of people charged with driving under the influence have blood tests. **In the Penrith area, practically 100 per cent.** So it is practicable to get blood tests for the vast majority under present conditions.

Mr Hanesman was a Macquarie Street Medical Specialist, and was a well-known campaigner for compulsory testing. Here, he raised two good arguments. He said that it was reasonable to introduce compulsion in stages. Then he gave some remarkable figures about the Penrith area. If they were accurate, then surely that argument, that there were not enough doctors, would not hold. **But were those figures correct?** Another doctor did not think so.

Letters, Dr P Bell, Penrith. I must object strongly to F.S. Hanesman's misconception of the facts about the availability of blood tests in Penrith.

The statement that 100 percent of persons arrested at Penrith for driving under the influence have blood tests is definitely not true. The local doctors rarely attend patients when requested by police. Only last night I declined such a request.

Doctors will continue to refuse to attend patients until they are regarded as professional witnesses in such cases, and not observers as they are at present – and in fact their observations carry less weight with magistrates than those of police witnesses.

I recently examined a well-known citizen of this area and he was not clinically under the influence of alcohol and I stated so in court, but because his blood alcohol was raised slightly no notice was taken of my evidence and the man was convicted. However, notice was taken of my observations in a higher court and his appeal was allowed.

My advice to all drivers is to refrain from having a blood test under the present circumstances, because even if an incorrect estimation of blood alcohol is made the magistrate will take notice of the result and not the doctor's evidence. I have had one case in which the level of blood alcohol as determined by the Government analyst was twice as high as that performed by an independent laboratory, and needless to say the higher figure was accepted by the Court.

I would suggest that the figure of 100 per cent tests done in Penrith is as much a true statement of fact as are many other unscientific statements which are made about the value of blood alcohol estimation as a true indication of sobriety.

Letters, SOLICITOR, Penrith. As a member of a legal firm engaged with drink-driving offences, I point out that the correct figure for the use of blood testing is not of the order of 100 per cent as Dr Hanesman claims. **Rather, it is less that 10 per cent**, and probably far lower. What might be true is that the police ask the driver if he wants a doctor, but the cases where a doctor attends is rare.

If the advocates for compulsory blood testing cannot be accurate in comparatively small matters such as this, how can they expect their opinions to be accepted on the broader aspects.

Letters, Dr B Iglegitzky. My attendance at the scene for drunk driving testing is only done if the subject agrees to submit to a blood test.

Too much emphasis has been laid on the drunken driver, and not enough on the innocent driver. He has had little to drink and it would be unjust to convict him of driving under the influence. That is, in my opinion, one of the main reasons for encouraging the use of blood tests. We should protect such drivers.

I, for one, am in favour of adopting the system in some of the USA, and having a standard of 0.15 p.c. blood alcohol as a minimum for conviction. Dr Hanesman does not agree with that, I know. If we were to adopt his standards, I am afraid that every second person who comes out of a hotel and enters his car would have to be arrested, and would most certainly be convicted, provided a sufficient number of doctors could be persuaded to participate.

In my experience, the driver who leaves no doubt of his sobriety at the time of examination – the truly drunken driver – invariably turns out to have had a reading of 0.15 at least. It takes a lot more to get a habitual drinker's level that high than in the case of an infrequent drinker. We then punish a man when he has had his usual quota and is quite capable of handling his vehicle.

Letters, F Hanesman, Macquarie Street, Sydney. The information, where I stated that nearly 100 per cent of cases in the Penrith district have blood tests, was given to me by a most responsible citizen from a full knowledge of the facts. I also adhere to my contention that there are facilities available in this State for blood samples to be taken in the majority of cases. Further, I have faith in the conscientiousness of the medical profession that few would refuse to examine, at his request, a person charged with drink-driving.

I can assure you that the results given by the Government Analyst can be accepted with every confidence, and I would completely agree with a magistrate in accepting the Analyst's result over that of an independent laboratory.

On the question of whose evidence is to be believed, I say that if it were generally accepted that the doctor's opinion was to outweigh other witnesses' evidence and the evidence of the blood test, it would mean in effect the end of the basis on which justice is at present conceived. The Court must surely find its verdict by an impartial consideration of all the evidence.

Letters, John Coutts. One of the main objections to the blood tests, where the police mandate the test would be taken, is that it is then **the police who administer the test**. Let me just say that the test operators then are not ethically and technically infallible.

Letters, A Small, Bendigo. Your Letters on drink-driving are ignoring all the important facts.

The Doctor's correspondents are happily assuming that it will be the medical profession who gets all the business. Why should this be so? **Anyone** can be trained for two days to take blood tests, and for another two to learn how to process them. We need professional Blood-Testers, good citizens who are available immediately to go to a collision. Doctors should not come into it. They should stay in their surgeries with their patients and stop running out to answer a "call from the police." It's all very dramatic, but people are getting sick of it.

Then there is the level of alcohol. We should start at a high level, and if that cuts the collision rate, society is smart enough to see what is happening, and will accept the gradual lowering of levels. No one is smart enough to pick the right level first up, and anyway, society has to be onside for new rules to last.

While we are at it, stop calling collisions "accidents." It might make the drivers involved feel better, but most "accidents" are certain to happen, whether it be today or tomorrow. Fast driving, heavy drinking, bad roads, and increasing number of cars ensure the dim-witted will have collisions. They are **certain** to – they are not accidents.

Mr Small raised some good points that have more or less come into effect since. But it took many years. Social change is always painfully slow.

Letters, B Hudson. I oppose compulsory blood tests for the same reason that I oppose any form of compulsion, until it has been shown to be for the good of the community, and good government. This includes compulsory voting, compulsory unionism, compulsory day-baking of bread, and compulsory closing of shops at arbitrary hours. I prefer freedom, a word in danger of being forgotten in our misnamed democracy.

Secondly, I oppose tests because I know, from a lifetime of personal observations, that some men may be irresponsible after one glass of beer, while others will be OK after six glasses. This alone would make any blood test useless.

Comment. The introduction of compulsory bloods tests has made big changes in society. My own impression is that most people do approve of the tests, more or less in their current form, though it still remains controversial as to whether the currents limits should be raised a bit. But the benefits of the new regime are so obvious that I suspect very few indeed would argue for the old days to return.

THE STUART DECISIONS

The Royal Commission reports. Stuart at last got a break at **the end of October**. The South Australian Government could see that the Royal Commission investigating his sentencing for murder would again be delayed. That meant his execution would need to be postponed. It argued that to force him to live for even more time in the shadow of the gallows was bordering on the inhumane, and therefore commuted his death sentence to one of life imprisonment.

The Royal Commission continued throughout the month of November. It was delayed a little by the difficulty in finding a replacement for the late Jim Shand. Then there were a large number of witnesses that had to be heard. The evidence from these witnesses proved to be somewhat confusing. Some of them said they had seen Stuart at some location at a certain time and others then said they had seen him somewhere else about the same time. It left the Commissioners with no clear indication of his guilt or innocence, and no clear signs of irregularity in his earlier trial. Accordingly, they found that the original decision of "guilty" should stand, and that Stuart should remain in prison.

He was held in gaol until 1973, then released. He then began a second life and became a respected tribal Arrente man, and the chairman of the Central Land Council. In Alice Springs, in the year 2000, **he presented the Queen with a painting** of the dreaming of his land, the Yeperenye or giant caterpillar.

A book by K Inglis, *The Stuart Case*, published in 2002, tells the story of his life. The film *Black and White*, produced by Louis Nowra, provides further insights into his life, and was also released in 2002.

ONE OPINION OF AUSTRALIA

Letters, C Carlsenson. If the Americans who recently arrived in Sydney seeking "the last bastion of freedom" decide to settle in this State, they will quickly find that they have left the frying-pan and landed in the fire.

Here, if they decide to work for a wage, their right to work will depend on obtaining a union ticket. They will then be forced to pay political levies or their right to work will be taken from them.

Here, if they decide to go into the retail or manufacturing business, they will have to obtain many and various permits and pay registration fees. They will also be told when they can open their place of business and also the hour they must close. The regulations, they will find, are often policed by agents provocateurs of the Shop Assistants' Union, who later share the fine imposed by the police magistrate.

Here, they will find it compulsory to vote at all elections, even though in some cases their only choice of candidates may be between a Socialist and a Communist.

Here, if they buy a rented house as a home for their family, they will be unable to get possession. They will find that by Act of Parliament the weekly tenancy has become a lease in perpetuity.

Here, whether farming or fishing, building or buying, shooting or shopping, all their actions will be controlled by Government inspectors and investigators, where they hoped to find freedom they will find bureaucratic bondage.

ONE LAST INNOVATION

Aromarama is coming to a theatre near you. The first motion picture with a smell had its world premiere in New York last night. The scent of oriental spices, incense, and night-club smoke wafted to the audience through an air-conditioning unit. The film "The Great Wall" uses a process called Aromarama, entering and leaving the theatre with the image on the screen. The high tech unit whisks the old smell out as soon as another is due.

Comment. They tried this in Sydney, but people said it stank.

NOW FOR SOME CHRISTMAS CHEER

It looked like a great Christmas for the shops. The year had been a good one economically for all concerned. Any one who wanted a job could get one. Travel, local and international, was on the increase, and cars were affordable for anyone who saved a bit, with the help of a burgeoning Hire Purchase industry. New families who wanted a house could also get one with a smallish deposit, and a biggish second mortgage. But the point here is that second mortgages **were** now available, and the stranglehold, that the banks had ruthlessly exercised on home lending, had been seriously weakened.

On top of that, wool had made something of a recovery, a minerals boom was just visible round the corner, and experts were warning about the dangers of the bloated stock market. There were no wars on the horizon, the Asians hordes that are often seen to be coming fast were now thought to be not coming at all, and the turkey was getting fat. **T'was indeed the Season to be jolly.**

Shoppers had plenty to choose from. For example, if you were into soft toys or dolls, these were among your options. The first, ferocious-looking one was actually set permanently on the wheeled frame. So, presumably, that you could push him round. The second one came complete with a feeding bottle, a powder spray, a sponge and, of course, a dummy. The third one, a panda, has now been done to death, but then was quite novel.

These toys, and lots of others, were advertised in the papers under the heading *CUDDLY TOYS FOR YOUR LITTLE CHERUBS.* It added that there were *several dolls that almost talk*.

The somewhat older children were in luck this year. Wyatt Earp was at that time stalking the TV, and these children thought he was just wonderful. So, parents were snapping up cowboy and cowgirl suits, especially the light leatherette types. The hats and weapons were indispensable side products. The Earp suits cost a little more than the sheriff suits, but the higher status of the former justified the price. Girls were well catered for, and the Annie Oakley suits cost the same as sheriffs' suits. These came with hats with blond plaits attached. There were also very efficient miniature toy rifles for the tiny tot's who wanted to share in the slaughter with their elder siblings.

Comment. Christmas for me, in these years, had its bad times. One of these was always Christmas morning. We only had three children of our own, but somehow by the time we came to open our presents under the tree, there were always ten or more of them yelling their heads off. One year we had three Asian kids that we had not seen before and never saw again.

But the noise of guns and drums and sirens and kazoos, and rapturous children, made this hour about the worst in the year for me. The worst thing of all, year after year, was the present that my thoughtful children had got for their Dad. I would slowly open it up, and surprise, surprise, there was a box of hankies. Oh Hell, not more, was my secret reaction.

I know that Mums got their share of Talcum Powder, and cute little bottles of Eau de Cologne, and that these too were received with as much grace as could be mustered. "It's the thought that counts", Mums always said, afterwards. But constant bruising will always leave marks. So please, if you were thinking of giving me some hankies for Christmas this year, I do thank you a lot, but would rather you didn't.

SUMMING UP 1959

I said earlier that this would not be a sensational year, and indeed it was not. Of course, there were the constant strikes, but nothing of great import. There was the magnified threat of the Red menace, but it was so small that I managed to spare you from it.

Apart from that, the nation was going well, and most families were busy and prosperous in a HP sort of way. The security blanket around the less fortunate saved them from the very worst, and most people had a smaller mortgage at the end of the year than at the beginning.

As for the future, things looked pretty good. The only exception would be the mid-Sixties when our young men were sent off the be killed for no good reason in Vietnam. That was a terrible few years, and was period hopefully we will never repeat.

Apart from that, our overseas trade has somehow kept the wolf from our door, our political system has had its downs and a few ups, but it was still the most stable in the world. We really have had a great run that has lasted more than half a century.

I hope and expect that this will continue. I hope too that you will continue to enjoy the (relative) paradise that we live in, and prosper at the same time as the nation does.

COMMENTS FROM READERS

Tom Lynch, Speers Point…..Some history writers make the mistake of trying to boost their authority by including graphs and charts all over the place. You on the other hand get a much better effect by saying things like "he made a pile". Or "every one worked hours longer that they should have, and felt like death warmed up at the end of the shift." I have seen other writers waste two pages of statistics painting the same picture as you did in a few words….

Barry Marr, Adelaide….you know that I am being facetious when I say that I wish the war had gone on for years longer so that you would have written more books about it…

Edna College, Auburn…. A few times I stopped and sobbed as you brought memories of the postman delivering letters, and the dread that ordinary people felt as he neared. How you captured those feelings yet kept your coverage from becoming maudlin or bogged down is a wonder to me….

Betty Kelly. Every time you seem to be getting serious you throw in a phrase or memory that lightens up the mood. In particular, in the war when you were describing the terrible carnage of Russian troops, for no reason, you ended with a ten line description of how aggrieved you felt and ended it with "apart from that, things are pretty good here". For me, it turned the unbearable into the bearable, and I went from feeling morbid and angry back to a normal human being….

Alan Davey, Brisbane….I particularly liked the light-hearted way you described the scenes at the airports as the American high-flying entertainers flew in. I had always seen the crowd behaviour as disgraceful, but your light-hearted description of it made me realise it was in fact harmless and just good fun….

MORE INFORMATION ON THESE BOOKS

Over the past 13 years the author, Ron Williams, has written this series of books that present a social history of Australia in the post-war period. They cover the period for 1939 to 1973, with one book for each year. Thus there are 35 books.

To capture the material for each book, the author, Ron Williams, worked his way through the *Sydney Morning Herald* and the *Age/Argus* day-by-day, and picked out the best stories, ideas and trivia. He then wrote them up into 176 pages of a year-book.

He writes in a direct conversational style, he has avoided statistics and charts, and has produced easily-read material that is entertaining, and instructive, and charming.

****

These books are available at all good book stores and retailers.

Chrissi and birthday books for Mum and Dad and Grans, and Aunt and Uncle and cousins and family and friends and work and everyone else.

Don't forget a good read and chuckle for yourself.

This series has 35 Year Books, from 1939 to 1973.

In 1962. Hitch-hiking was still safe for all concerned, and the wonders of The Pill were being extolled. And condemned. Terylene swimsuits for men were being exposed, there were some people who were suggesting that a link between smoking and cancer of the lung. Many people were concerned that we were being Americanised. They would prefer the current Pommification. Most people still hated the Japs, but there were occasional voices urging acceptance

In 1963, the bodies of Bogle and Chandler mystified police and still do so. The Queen popped in and knighted Bob, now Sir Bob Menzies. Initiation ceremonies to universities and the military vexed some caring mothers, and the Labour Party was ridiculed for listening to 36 faceless men. The fruits of the Baby Boom were being harvested so that hooliganism was a big problem. A learned professor suggested that this fair land should take in 50,000 negroes as migrants. John Kennedy, President of the USA, was shot dead.